Reuters News Agency Reports on Our World

ロイターで学ぶ、環境、健康、AI、サイエンス

Shinji Ogasawara　Ako Okuda　Akira Hiroe　William Collins

EIHŌSHA

まえがき

　長年、大学で英語の授業を担当していて、多くの学生から「英語のニュースを聞き取れるようになりたい」、さらには「英語を国際語として使いこなせるようになりたい」のような声をよく聞きます。本書はそのような要求に応えるために、ロイター通信社が配信した、生の英語を教材として使用し、様々なタスクを用意した教科書です。英語を使いこなせるようになるため、4技能の養成を意識し、統合型の教科書として工夫を凝らしたタスクをたくさん用意しています。また、英語学習が楽しく進められるように、ロイター通信社の配信したニュースの中から、学生のみなさんが関心を持ちそうな、環境、健康、AI、サイエンスの分野をターゲットとし、楽しく学べる内容を中心に厳選しました。またニュースは1分半から2分半程度の短めの長さのものを中心に選んであります。教科書には学習用のDVDも付属されていますので、何度も視聴し、英語の学習を進めるとともに、現代の社会のニュースを楽しんでください。そして、学習のためのタスクは、以下のものを用意しています。

Task 1. Guessing & Skimming: 写真とKey Wordsを見て内容を推測します。

Task 2. Matching: Key Wordsの意味の確認のため、該当する英語による説明文を選択肢から選びます（Key Wordsは、ニュースの中で使用されたものを選んでいますので、ニュースのリスニングやリーディングの際にも役に立ちます）。

Task 3. Viewing & Scanning: 動画を視聴して、内容の質問に対する適切な答えを選びます。

Task 4. Dictation: 音声（動画）を聞いて、下線の部分にチャンク（英語数語）を書き入れて、テキストを完成します。

Task 5. Reading: Words & Phrasesを参考にして、テキスト全体を読み、より深い内容の質問に、日本語で答えます。

Task 6. Summary: テキストの内容に関して、100語程度の英文サマリーを完成します。用意されたパラグラフの中に、適切な英語1語を書き入れます。

Task 7. Writing & Speaking: 本文やTask 6のSummaryを参考にして、テキストで使用された英単語やフレーズも利用しながら、同じようなテーマの英文を数行で書いてみます。また、時間があるときは、書いたものを発表してみましょう。

　教科書のタスクの前半は、語彙やリスニングの学習が中心です。本書で使用する音源は、実際のニュースで使用されたものです。これが聞き取れるようになることが、まず実践的な英語能力を高める第一歩です。そのためには、英語のリスニング訓練において、「authentic」

なノイズ入りの教材に挑戦しなければなりません。この場合のノイズとは、周りの騒音はもちろんのこと、発音のくせや文法のみだれ、声の強弱、異文化に由来する価値観の違いなど、コミュニケーションを妨げるものすべてを言います。このような英語に慣れることや聞き取れるようになることが大切です。ノイズのないリスニング教材をいくら聞いても、実践で役にたつリスニング力は養成されません。

　タスクの後半は、リーディングやライティングを中心とした活動です。前半 Task 4 のディテーションを終了すると、テキスト全体が完成します。Task 5 は、質問の答えを探しながら、全体を読む活動です。前半のリスニング活動ではうまく聞き取れなかったところや理解が難しかった部分などは、文章をじっくり読みながら確認作業をし、質問に対して答えを日本語で完成します。それにより、ニュースの内容をより深く理解することができます。後半の Task 6 や Task 7 では、ニュースを要約する活動やニュースに関連したテーマで英語を数行書く活動が用意されています。書いたものをだれかに伝える活動をすれば、スピーキングの練習にもなります。

　本書を利用して、大学生のみなさんが、実践的で4技能のバランスのとれた英語力を身につけることを期待します。また、英語学習を通して、今世界でどのような変化が起こっているのか、ロイター通信社のニュースで学習しましょう。

　最後に、本書の出版や編集において、数々のアドバイスをいただき、完成に向けてご尽力いただきました、英宝社社長佐々木元氏と編集長佐藤貴博氏に、心よりお礼申し上げます。

2024 年秋

著者代表

小笠原　真司

目 次

Unit 1.
Snow Lacking, French Ski Resort Turns to New Activities
2

Unit 2.
Can This Spoon Help Japanese People Eat Less Salt?
8

Unit 3.
This Robot Can Predict a Smile Before It Happens
14

Unit 4.
Telecom Boxes Are Becoming EV Charging Stations in Britain
20

Unit 5.
This Is What the Future of Medicine Looks Like
26

Unit 6.
UK Toddler Regains Hearing in Gene Therapy Breakthrough
32

Unit 7.
This AI 'Turtle' Soup Is Helping the Endangered Species
38

Unit 8.
EU: Ocean Temperature Hit Record High in February
44

Unit 9.
This Florida Shark Prof Wants Girls to Dive into Science
50

Unit 10.
Pig-to-human Kidney Transplant Success May Offer Hope
56

Unit 11.
Researchers Make Medical Tests from Used Chewing Gum
62

Unit 12.
Seaweed Microrobots Could One Day Treat Cancer, Researcher Says
68

Unit 13.
Brazil Braces for Worst Coral Bleaching Ever
74

Unit 14.
Researchers Uncover 'Phonetic Alphabet' of Sperm Whales
80

Unit 15.
New Zealand's Space Industry Shoots for the Stars
86

Key Words List
93

Reuters News Agency Reports on Our World

――ロイターで学ぶ、環境、健康、AI、サイエンス――

Snow Lacking, French Ski Resort Turns to New Activities

YouTube

Task 1 (Guessing & Skimming)

動画を視聴する前に、写真と Key Words を見て内容を推測してみましょう。推測した内容をペアで話し合ってみましょう。

Key Words
1. resort
2. snow
3. activities
4. climate change
5. tourists
6. businesses
7. survival
8. economic impacts
9. adapt
10. Hautacam

Task 2 (Matching)

Key Words の内容を表している英語を下の選択肢A~Jより選び、Key Words の意味を確認しましょう。

1. resort (　　)
2. snow (　　)
3. activities (　　)
4. climate change (　　)
5. tourists (　　)
6. businesses (　　)
7. survival (　　)
8. economic impacts (　　)
9. adapt (　　)
10. Hautacam (　　)

❏ 選択肢 ❏

A. The process by which the Earth's weather patterns are changing
B. The act of managing to continue to exist or operate despite difficulties
C. The name of a specific ski resort in the French Pyrenees
D. People who travel for pleasure or culture
E. Things that people do for enjoyment or entertainment
F. A place for relaxation or recreation, often for vacations
G. To change or adjust something to fit new conditions or environments
H. Frozen precipitation in the form of white flakes
I. The effects or consequences that events, policies, or changes have on the economy
J. Commercial operations or establishments

Task 3 (Viewing & Scanning: Answer the Multiple-Choice Questions)

動画を視聴し、次の質問の答えを、A~Dより選びましょう。

1: What type of snow is used at Hautacam Ski Resort?
  A) Natural snow
  B) Artificial snow
  C) Both A and B
  D) Neither

2: How often did the resort open in the current year?
  A) Every weekend
  B) Only two days
  C) Every day
  D) None

3: What is the main concern for local businesses due to lack of snow?
   A) Lack of tourists
   B) Increased costs
   C) Overcrowding
   D) None of the above

4: What is the main alternative activity mentioned?
   A) Climbing
   B) Snowboarding
   C) Zip line biking
   D) Ice skating

Task 4 (Dictation)

動画を音声に注意して視聴し、下線の部分にチャンク（英語数語）を書き込みましょう。

It's not the typical ski resort experience. Bikes on zip line and outdoor rides. Here in the French Pyrenees, a recurring [1] .... means uncertain times for businesses that revolve around ski hills. And while tourists may still remark at the view . . . .

"C'est super!" It's left resort staff wondering about their livelihood.
Marie-Florentine Hulin: "In the future, will this become the only recipe for our resort in winter? I don't know, [2] ...."

Marie-Florentine Hulin is the marketing and communications manager of the Hautacam Ski Resorts in Beaucens, where they've opted [3] ....
.... machines.

"We usually have heavy snowfalls in January, which allows us to open the four weeks of February. This year, there is really no snow at all. We only opened our [4] .... Maybe next year, we will have a meter of snow in January, which will allow us [5] .... of the ski resort being open. But we are still going with trends, which are still about the scarcity of snow, in the end."

But while visitors are enjoying the alternative activities . . . warming weather systems and a [6].. are testing the survival of a myriad of businesses. The local ski school is closed and ski rental shops are seeing fewer customers.

Josiane Sempe owns a rental shop in the area.
"If we keep having seasons like this one, we'll [7]..
We won't be able to go on. We'll need to think of something else."

France's public audit office warned this month that, in the face of climate change, most resorts were likely to feel the [8].., with areas south of the Alps hit hardest.

At Hautacam's restaurant, visitors eat lunch outdoors, while server Leo Villoint tries to keep a positive attitude.
"We feel like we're not in control, that we're losing the snow little by little and that the coming years [9].., so we try to find other things."

Residents like Stephane Remy are taking a pragmatic approach.
"The snow situation is likely to get worse, we know that. So we might as well adapt ourselves to this and find other [10].. such as cycling or hiking."

Snow Lacking, French Ski Resort Turns to New Activities

Task 5 (Reading: Answer the Questions in Japanese)

Task 4 で完成した英語ニュースを読んで、次の質問に日本語で答えましょう。Words & Phrases も参考にしましょう。

Words & Phrases

the French Pyrenees　フランスのピレネー山脈／recurring　繰り返し発生する／Beaucens　ボース（フランス中北部、パリの南西に広がる地方）／scarcity　不足、欠乏／myriad　無数／in the face of　（困難などに）直面して／pragmatic　実践的な

1. リゾートのスタッフは、将来についてどのような感情を抱いていますか。

   ....
   ....

2. このスキー場のスタッフたちが、質問1のように思っている原因は何ですか。

   ....
   ....

3. Beaucens の Hautacam スキーリゾートは、スキー場として雪に関してどのような選択をしましたか。

   ....
   ....

4. フランスの公的監査機関によると、気候変動の影響を一番受ける地域はどこですか。

   ....
   ....

5. Stephane Remy は、状況が悪化する中、どうするべきだと言っていますか。

   ....
   ....

Task 6 (Summary)

かっこに英語１語を入れて、動画ニュースの内容をまとめましょう。なお、ヒントになるよう、最初の文字を指定しています。

Words & Phrases
threaten 脅かす／strive 奮闘する、努力する／sustain 維持する

At the Hautacam Ski [R   ] in the French Pyrenees, a lack of snow due to climate change is threatening the survival of local [b   ]. With tourists declining and the economy suffering, the resort is adapting by offering alternative [a   ] like zip-lining and biking instead of traditional skiing. While ski schools and rental shops [f   ] challenges, Hautacam aims to attract visitors through these new offerings. Locals are pursuing adaptation by promoting activities such as [c   ] and hiking, striving to sustain their livelihoods in the face of environmental changes.

Task 7 (Writing & Speaking)

本文や Task 6 を参考にして、気候変動について、自由に英語で数行書いてみましょう。また、ペアで発表をしてみましょう。

....
....
....
....
....

Unit 2 Can This Spoon Help Japanese People Eat Less Salt?

Task 1 (Guessing & Skimming)

動画を視聴する前に、写真と Key Words を見て内容を推測してみましょう。推測した内容をペアで話し合ってみましょう。

Key Words
1. electric field
2. utensil
3. rechargeable battery
4. reduce salt intake
5. consumption
6. perceived saltiness
7. high blood pressure
8. dietary habits
9. limited run
10. global users

Task 2 (Matching)

Key Words の内容を表している英語を下の選択肢 A~J より選び、Key Words の意味を確認しましょう。

1. electric field (　　)
2. utensil (　　)
3. rechargeable battery (　　)
4. reduce salt intake (　　)
5. consumption (　　)
6. perceived saltiness (　　)
7. high blood pressure (　　)
8. dietary habits (　　)
9. limited run (　　)
10. global users (　　)

❏ 選択肢 ❏

A. To lower the amount of salt consumed in one's diet
B. A condition where the force of the blood against the artery walls is too high
C. The act of using up or consuming a substance
D. A special offer available for a limited time
E. Usual ways of preparing and consuming food
F. People from different parts of the world
G. The way in which something salty is understood or interpreted
H. A tool used for cooking, eating or other tasks
I. The process by which electric forces are applied
J. Electrical storage device that can be filled again with energy

Task 3 (Viewing & Scanning: Answer the Multiple-Choice Questions)

動画を視聴し、次の質問の答えを、A~D より選びましょう。

1. What is the purpose of the Electric Salt Spoon?
   A) To weigh the food being consumed
   B) To store sodium ions
   C) To enhance the salty taste without adding more salt
   D) To increase the electric charge on food

2. Who co-developed the Electric Salt Spoon?
   A) A researcher at Kirin
   B) Ai Sato
   C) A nutritionist at Meiji University
   D) Homei Miyashita

3. What health issue is linked to excess sodium intake according to the article?
   A) Diabetes
   B) Heart attacks
   C) Obesity
   D) High blood pressure and strokes

4. What is Kirin's goal for the Electric Salt Spoon within five years?
   A) To sell 200 spoons
   B) To have 1 million users globally
   C) To sell it exclusively in Japan
   D) To start sales overseas

Task 4 (Dictation)

動画を音声に注意して視聴し、下線の部分にチャンク（英語数語）を書き込みましょう。

This Electric Salt Spoon can apparently enhance salty tastes.
Researchers hope it can help users [1]＿＿＿＿＿＿＿＿＿＿ on sodium consumption and promote a [2]＿＿＿＿＿＿＿＿＿＿.

[3]＿＿＿＿＿＿＿＿＿＿ Japanese drinks giant Kirin Holdings, the utensil works by passing a weak electric field to concentrate the sodium ion molecules [4]＿＿＿＿＿＿＿＿＿＿. This enhances the perceived saltiness of the food. Weighing [5]＿＿＿＿＿＿＿＿＿＿, the spoon runs on a rechargeable lithium battery.

Meiji University professor Homei Miyashita co-developed the utensil.
"When you're eating low-salt foods some of that sodium comes into contact with your tongue but not all, so we use an electric current to attract the sodium to the tongue. Once you do that, lots of sodium is drawn to the tongue and gives the impression of a saltier flavor."

Excess sodium intake [6]＿＿＿＿＿＿＿＿＿＿ increased incidence of high blood pressure, strokes and other ailments. Kirin says the technology has [7]＿＿＿＿＿＿＿＿＿＿ in Japan, where the average adult consumes about 10 grams of salt [8]＿＿＿＿＿＿＿＿＿＿. That's double the amount recommended by the World Health Organization.

Ai Sato is a researcher at Kirin:

"Overall, Japanese people need to reduce their salt intake but it can be very hard to change the diet we're used to. We created this Electric Salt tool so they can adjust their salt intake and get used to lighter-tasting meals."

Kirin plans to sell 200 of its Electric Salt Spoons online for roughly $127 apiece in May and a [9]... at a Japanese retailer in June. The company is hoping for [10]... within five years. Sales overseas will start in 2025.

Task 5 (Reading: Answer the Questions in Japanese)

Task 4 で完成した英語ニュースを読んで、次の質問に日本語で答えましょう。Words & Phrases も参考にしましょう。

Words & Phrases

enhance 強化する／sodium ion ナトリウムイオン／molecule 分子／electric current 電流／stroke 脳卒中／ailment 病気／the World Health Organization 世界保健機関／retailer 小売店

1. 電気塩スプーンは、どのようにして塩分の知覚を強化しますか。

   ....
   ....

2. どこの大学のだれが、この器具の開発に関与していますか。

   ....
   ....

3. 過剰なナトリウム摂取が関連している健康問題は何ですか。

   ....
   ....

4. なぜキリンはこの技術の重要性を強調していますか。

   ....
   ....

5. 電気塩スプーンの販売計画には、どのようなものがありますか。

   ....
   ....

Task 6 (Summary)

かっこに英語1語を入れて、動画ニュースの内容をまとめましょう。なお、ヒントになるよう、最初の文字を指定しています。

Japanese company Kirin Holdings has developed an Electric Salt Spoon that enhances the perceived saltiness of food by using an [e   ] field to concentrate sodium ions on the tongue. Powered by a rechargeable [b   ], the spoon aims to reduce sodium consumption and promote health by helping users lower their salt intake, thereby decreasing the risk of high blood [p   ]. Kirin plans a limited [r   ] of 200 spoons in Japan, hoping to reach global users by 2025. This utensil allows people to maintain their dietary [h   ] while consuming less sodium.

Task 7 (Writing & Speaking)

本文やTask 6を参考にして、日本人の健康について、自由に英語で数行書いてみましょう。また、ペアで発表をしてみましょう。

....
....
....
....
....

Unit 3 This Robot Can Predict a Smile Before It Happens

YouTube

Task 1 (Guessing & Skimming)

動画を視聴する前に、写真と Key Words を見て内容を推測してみましょう。推測した内容をペアで話し合ってみましょう。

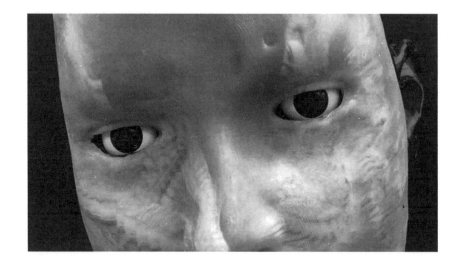

Key Words

1. anticipate
2. facial expressions
3. intuitive
4. AI (artificial intelligence)
5. AI models
6. silicone skin
7. high-resolution cameras
8. self-modeling
9. nonverbal communication
10. facial actuators

....

....

....

....

Task 2 (Matching)

Key Words の内容を表している英語を下の選択肢 A~J より選び、Key Words の意味を確認しましょう。

1. anticipate (　)
2. facial expressions (　)
3. intuitive (　)
4. AI (artificial intelligence) (　)
5. AI models (　)
6. silicone skin (　)
7. high-resolution cameras (　)
8. self-modeling (　)
9. nonverbal communication (　)
10. facial actuators (　)

❏ 選択肢 ❏

A. The practice of a robot learning from its own movements to understand its mechanisms
B. To expect or predict something and prepare for it in advance
C. Cameras that capture detailed images, enhancing the quality of interaction
D. Synthetic material that mimics human skin, used to cover robotic parts
E. Technology concerned with building smart machines capable of performing tasks that typically require human intelligence
F. Physical components in robots that simulate human muscle movements to make facial expressions
G. Understanding or knowing something instinctively, without the need for conscious reasoning
H. Artificial intelligence programs that analyze and react to visual data
I. Expressions made by the face that communicate emotional states
J. Communication that occurs through means other than spoken words

Task 3 (Viewing & Scanning: Answer the Multiple-Choice Questions)

動画を視聴し、次の質問の答えを、A~D より選びましょう。

1. What enables Emo to mimic human facial expressions?
   A) Audio sensors
   B) Motion sensors
   C) Actuators in its face
   D) Light sensors

2. Why is the silicone skin important for Emo?
   A) It makes the robot waterproof.
   B) It collects solar power.
   C) It gives the robot a more lifelike appearance.
   D) It helps the robot detect heat.

3. Which AI capability is NOT mentioned as part of Emo's functions?
   A) Mimicking vocal tones
   B) Detecting human faces
   C) Anticipating facial expressions
   D) Controlling facial actuators

4. How does Emo 'learn' to improve its expressions according to the article?
   A) Through feedback from users
   B) By updating its software via the internet
   C) By observing human interactions
   D) By self-modeling in front of a camera

Task 4 (Dictation)

動画を音声に注意して視聴し、下線の部分にチャンク（英語数語）を書き込みましょう。

This AI-integrated robotic face can [1]... before it happens. It's called Emo and it can anticipate and mimic human facial expressions.

Engineers at Columbia University's Creative Machines Lab say they believe it is a [2].. in improving interaction quality and fostering trust between humans and robots.

Through advancements like ChatGPT, many robots have made strides in verbal communication. But their [3].. and express facial cues has lagged.

(Yuhang Hu, PhD candidate, Columbia University)
"So robots become more advanced and complicated like those powered by AI models, there's a growing need to make these interactions more intuitive." This is Yuhang Hu, a PhD student at the Creative Machines Lab.

"Emo [4]_____ several AI models including detect human faces, controlling facial actuators to mimic facial expressions and even anticipating human facial expressions. This allows Emo to interact in a way that feels timely and genuine." Emo's human-like head [5]_____ for a range of facial expressions and [6]_____ soft, silicone skin. It features high-resolution cameras in its eyes for lifelike interactions and eye contact, [7]_____ nonverbal communication. The robot was trained using a process termed "self-modeling," wherein Emo made random movements in front of a camera, [8]_____ between its facial expressions and motor commands. It was then shown videos of human expressions.

A study published in Science Robotics described Emo as [9]_____ _____ human facial expressions and mimic them simultaneously, even predicting a forthcoming smile. Hu is the study's lead author.
"Our next step involves integrating verbal communication capabilities. [10]_____ _____ in more complex and natural conversations."

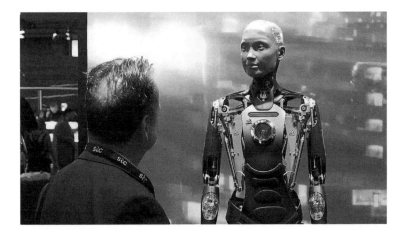

Task 5 (Reading: Answer the Questions in Japanese)

Task 4 で完成した英語ニュースを読んで、次の質問に日本語で答えましょう。Words & Phrases も参考にしましょう。

Words & Phrases

AI-integrated AI 統合型の／**mimic** 模倣する／**interaction** 相互作用、やりとり／**make strides** 進歩を遂げる／**verbal communication** 言葉によるコミュニケーション／**lag** 立ち遅れる／**detect** 検出する／**simultaneously** 同時に／**forthcoming** 出現する

1. ChatGPT などの進歩により、多くのロボットは verbal communication の点では進歩をしていますが、どのような点の改良がまだ遅れていると言っていますか。

   ....
   ....

2. Emo は人間の表情をどのようにして予測し、模倣することができますか。

   ....
   ....

3. Emo の顔の表情を制御するために使用されるアクチュエータは、何個ありますか。

   ....
   ....

4. Emo は顔の表情の訓練を、どのようにして行っていますか。

   ....
   ....

5. Emo の次のチャレンジは、どのようなことですか。

   ....
   ....

Task 6 (Summary)

かっこに英語1語を入れて、動画ニュースの内容をまとめましょう。なお、ヒントになるよう、最初の文字を指定しています。

Words & Phrases
enhance　〜を高める、向上させる／ feature　特徴として持っている

Engineers at Columbia University have developed Emo, an AI-integrated robotic face that uses predictive technology and AI models to [a　　　] and mimic human facial expressions, enhancing intuitive [i　　　] between humans and robots. Emo features 26 facial actuators covered with silicone skin, and its eyes contain high-resolution [c　　　] for lifelike interactions and eye contact, crucial for [n　　　] communication. Trained through a process called self-modeling, Emo can predict a forthcoming smile, marking a significant advancement in [a　　　] intelligence and human-robot relationships.

Task 7 (Writing & Speaking)

本文やTask 6を参考にして、AIロボットができることについて、自由に英語で数行書いてみましょう。また、ペアで発表をしてみましょう。

Unit 4　Telecom Boxes Are Becoming EV Charging Stations in Britain

YouTube

Task 1　(Guessing & Skimming)

動画を視聴する前に、写真と Key Words を見て内容を推測してみましょう。推測した内容をペアで話し合ってみましょう。

Key Words

1. telecom boxes
2. electric vehicle
3. telecom giant
4. redundant
5. reuse
6. charging stations
7. range anxiety
8. availability
9. expand
10. run the trial

Task 2 (Matching)

Key Words の内容を表している英語を下の選択肢A~Jより選び、Key Words の意味を確認しましょう。

1. telecom boxes (　)
2. electric vehicle (　)
3. telecom giant (　)
4. redundant (　)
5. reuse (　)
6. charging stations (　)
7. range anxiety (　)
8. availability (　)
9. expand (　)
10. run the trial (　)

❏ 選択肢 ❏

- A. Anxiety experienced by electric vehicle drivers regarding the sufficiency of their vehicle's battery range
- B. A very large and influential company in the telecommunications industry
- C. No longer needed or useful, often because something else can perform the same function
- D. Cabinets traditionally used for housing telecommunications equipment
- E. To use something again, often for a different purpose, instead of throwing it away
- F. A place equipped with facilities where electric vehicles can be charged
- G. To increase in size, number or importance
- H. To conduct or carry out a test or an experiment to evaluate its effectiveness or performance
- I. Energy-driven vehicles that operate without conventional fuels
- J. The state of being able to be used or obtained; being accessible or ready for use

Task 3 (Viewing & Scanning: Answer the Multiple-Choice Questions)

動画を視聴し、次の質問の答えを、A~Dより選びましょう。

1. What is the primary purpose of transforming telecom boxes into EV charging stations?
   A) To provide free internet access
   B) To reduce urban clutter
   C) To repurpose existing infrastructure for environmental benefits
   D) To increase property values

2. What is the main goal of reusing telecom boxes according to Jess Kyte, the second woman in the video?
   A) To increase broadband speeds
   B) To enhance the beauty of city streets
   C) To contribute towards net zero
   D) To promote the use of electric vehicles

3. What percentage of British drivers said they would own an EV if charging were easier?
   A) About 14%   B) About 24%
   C) About 40%   D) About 50%

4. How many trial sites is BT considering for their pilot project across the UK?
   A) 5400   B) 2030
   C) 540   D) 600

Task 4 (Dictation)

動画を音声に注意して視聴し、下線の部分にチャンク（英語数語）を書き込みましょう。

British telecom boxes are being transformed into electric vehicle charging stations. The green cabinets are a common sight on British streets. They store broadband and phone cables for telecom giant BT, but are [1]_____ as the company rolls out fibre. So the idea behind a new pilot project is to make the green boxes, [2]_____.

(Jess Kyte, Product Director, Etc. at BT Group)
"This seemed like a really good opportunity to reuse the points of power, reuse some existing street furniture and help contribute towards that drive towards net zero."

Craig Wright is an EV driver who lives in Haddington, Scotland. He knows all too well the worry that can come from [3]_____ to charge.

"I think that when you're planning a journey, especially a long-distance journey, it helps to have provision. So, that's the main thing. Driving an EV is kind of range anxiety, not knowing if you're going to get a charge to get back home and that sort of thing."

And he's not alone. BT says its research shows some British drivers don't want to go electric because of [4] _____ charging stations.

[5] _____ they'd have an EV already if charging were less of an issue.

There were [6] _____ charge points across the UK at the end of last year, according to figures quoted by BT from Zapmap. But the government wants to boost that number to 300,000 [7] _____.

BT's start-up incubation hub, called Etc., is running the cabinet trial. This is its first charge point . . . and residents can [8] _____ until the end of May.

Information about pricing, availability and charging speeds is available on an app.
"Well, we know we've got to expand EV charging . . . ."
Fiona Hyslop is Scotland's cabinet secretary for transport. She says it will help EV drivers outside of cities.

"We know that we can get EV chargers in town centers, actually on the periphery of towns that can be the best place that people can go so they don't have to go somewhere else to charge their car."

BT is planning to [9] _____ into the English county of West Yorkshire next. It's eyeing [10] _____ across the UK.

Task 5 (Reading: Answer the Questions in Japanese)

Task 4で完成した英語ニュースを読んで、次の質問に日本語で答えましょう。Words & Phrases も参考にしましょう。

Words & Phrases
roll out を展開する／**net zero** ネットゼロ（温室効果ガスの排出量を、排出量から森林吸収量等を差し引いた合計でゼロにすること）／**issue** 問題／**boost** 増やす／**incubation** 案、企て／**cabinet secretary for transport** 交通担当閣僚／**periphery** 周辺／**the English county of West Yorkshire** ウェストヨークシャー州

1. 環境保護のための取り組みとして、電気通信ボックスをどのように利用していますか。

2. 充電ステーションの設置によって、解決しようとしている主な問題は何ですか。

3. BT がこのプロジェクトで用意している充電ポイントの利用は、いつまで無料ですか。

4. Fiona Hyslop は、このプロジェクトにどのような期待を寄せていますか。

5. このプロジェクトの拡張について、BT はどのような計画を持っていますか。

Task 6 (Summary)

かっこに英語1語を入れて、動画ニュースの内容をまとめましょう。なお、ヒントになるよう、最初の文字を指定しています。

Words & Phrases

rollout 発売、初公開／ **alleviate** （問題を）軽減する、緩和する／ **infrastructure** インフラ（水道、電気、鉄道、道路などの社会的基本施設）

British telecom giant BT is transforming redundant telecom [b   ] into electric vehicle charging stations as part of a [g   ] initiative to promote EV adoption and [s   ]. These green cabinets, once used for broadband and phone cables, are becoming redundant technology due to the rollout of fiber. By repurposing them, BT aims to alleviate range [a   ] among EV drivers by increasing the number of charging stations. Their startup hub, Etc., is piloting this project with plans to expand to 600 sites [a   ] the UK, supporting government targets for EV infrastructure.

Task 7 (Writing & Speaking)

本文やTask 6を参考にして、電気自動車のことについて、自由に英語で数行書いてみましょう。また、ペアで発表をしてみましょう。

....

....

....

....

....

Unit 5 This Is What the Future of Medicine Looks Like

YouTube

Task 1 (Guessing & Skimming)

動画を視聴する前に、写真と Key Words を見て内容を推測してみましょう。推測した内容をペアで話し合ってみましょう。

Key Words

1. robotic
2. surgery
3. cutting-edge
4. technology
5. healthcare
6. high-precision
7. safety
8. diagnostic
9. wearable
10. Mobile World Congress

Task 2 (Matching)

Key Words の内容を表している英語を下の選択肢 A~J より選び、Key Words の意味を確認しましょう。

1. robotic (　)
2. surgery (　)
3. cutting-edge (　)
4. technology (　)
5. healthcare (　)
6. high-precision (　)
7. safety (　)
8. diagnostic (　)
9. wearable (　)
10. Mobile World Congress (　)

❑ 選択肢 ❑

A. Relating to the identification of a problem, especially in medical or technical contexts
B. Operated by machines or robots, not manually
C. Very advanced, modern, or innovative
D. The application of scientific knowledge for practical purposes
E. The condition of being protected from or unlikely to cause danger, risk, or injury
F. Medical procedures involving incisions with instruments; performed to repair damage or arrest disease in a living body
G. An annual trade show dedicated to mobile and related industries
H. Small electronic devices that can be worn on the body as implants or accessories
I. The maintenance and improvement of physical and mental health
J. It is very accurate or exact, with minimal errors

Task 3 (Viewing & Scanning: Answer the Multiple-Choice Questions)

動画を視聴し、次の質問の答えを、A~D より選びましょう。

1: What type of feedback does the surgical robot provide?
 A) Emotional feedback
 B) Sensory feedback
 C) Visual feedback
 D) Auditory feedback

2: Where was the health technology displayed?
   A) CES in Las Vegas
   B) IFA in Berlin
   C) Mobile World Congress in Barcelona
   D) TechCrunch Disrupt in San Francisco

3: What type of medical condition can the new wearable technology diagnose?
   A) Diabetes   B) Stroke
   C) Cancer   D) Heart disease

4: What is a concern regarding AI in healthcare?
   A) Cost   B) Accuracy
   C) Ethical issues   D) Speed

Task 4 (Dictation)

動画を音声に注意して視聴し、下線の部分にチャンク（英語数語）を書き込みましょう。

This is an AI-assisted high-precision surgical robot. It applies [1]... to the surgeon during critical moments of surgery, and is one of the many cutting-edge health technologies [2]... at the Mobile World Congress fair in Barcelona this year.

"Now we are talking about robotic surgery, but the next future is the 'digital surgery.'"

Tech companies are fighting for their spot in medicine and the talk of the town this year—is [3]... .

Jaume Amat Riera is the CEO and founder of Rob Surgical.
"One of the main weaknesses of the robotics is that the surgeons, they cannot work with sensory feedback because they are managing the instruments with their control from the console. So with our new artificial intelligence tools we provide

to them this sensory feedback to the surgeon, so the surgeon can feel when they are touching the tissues."

He said the combination of robotics AI tools and diagnostic imaging would [4]..—and precision. Other companies are looking to wearable tech. [5].. where a patient has a stroke, this headband can instantly monitor their brain status. For medical technicians—these AR glasses bring specialists from [6].. into their ambulances.

"We have AR glasses on the emergency medical technician, so he can do a [7].. with a doctor or surgeon on the way to the hospital to [8].. on how to treat the patient. And he also can see—or she —can see vital signs of heartbeat and blood pressure in those glasses so he doesn't have to [9].. ."

Companies are hoping the buzz around AI will boost business prospects. Many here would argue its application in the healthcare sector can improve medical capacities and offer advantages to both, staff and patients. But many experts caution AI technology can raise [10].. concerns.

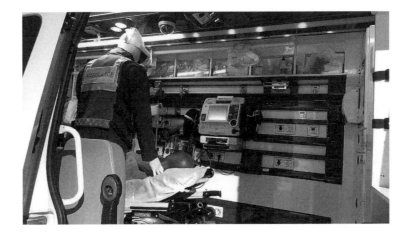

Task 5 (Reading: Answer the Questions in Japanese)

Task 4 で完成した英語ニュースを読んで、次の質問に日本語で答えましょう。Words & Phrases も参考にしましょう。

Words & Phrases

surgeon 外科医／**critical moments** 重要な瞬間／**talk of the town** その話題でもちきり／**CEO** 最高経営責任者／**founder** 創立者／**console** コンソール（外科医が手術用の器具を操作するための制御装置や操作パネルのこと）／**tissue** 組織／**heartbeat** 心拍数／**blood pressure** 血圧／**the buzz around AI** AI の話題

1. Jaume Amat Riera が紹介している人口頭脳ツールを用いると、外科医はどのような利点がありますか。

   ....

   ....

2. 医療で使用される AI は、主にどのような点を向上させますか。

   ....

   ....

3. どのような技術が、救急車の中のような緊急医療で活用されると言っていますか。

   ....

   ....

4. 質問 3 の技術を使用すれば、救急車の中でもどのようなことが可能になりますか。

   ....

   ....

5. 医療分野での AI の懸念事項は何ですか。

   ....

   ....

Task 6 (Summary)

かっこに英語1語を入れて、動画ニュースの内容をまとめましょう。なお、ヒントになるよう、最初の文字を指定しています。

Words & Phrases
address 〈問題〉と取り組む、対処する／showcase ～をPRする、～を売り込む

At the Mobile World Congress in Barcelona, [c   ] healthcare technologies are on display, including an AI-assisted high-precision surgical robot that provides sensory feedback to surgeons during critical moments of [s   ]. Jaume Amat Riera, CEO of Rob Surgical, says their innovation addresses a key weakness in robotic surgery by [a   ] surgeons to feel when they are touching tissues. Other companies are showcasing [w   ] technology, like headbands that monitor brain status in stroke patients and AR glasses that assist medical technicians. While artificial intelligence promises significant advancements in healthcare, experts warn of potential legal and ethical [c   ].

Task 7 (Writing & Speaking)

本文やTask 6を参考にして、AIができることで人が助かることについて、自由に英語で数行書いてみましょう。また、ペアで発表をしてみましょう。

Unit 6 UK Toddler Regains Hearing in Gene Therapy Breakthrough

YouTube

Task 1 (Guessing & Skimming)

動画を視聴する前に、写真と Key Words を見て内容を推測してみましょう。推測した内容をペアで話し合ってみましょう。

Key Words

1. toddler
2. deaf
3. regain
4. gene therapy
5. mind-blown
6. groundbreaking
7. combat
8. one and done
9. cochlear implants
10. obstacles

....

....

....

Task 2 (Matching)

Key Words の内容を表している英語を下の選択肢A~Jより選び、Key Words の意味を確認しましょう。

1. toddler ( )
2. deaf ( )
3. regain ( )
4. gene therapy ( )
5. mind-blown ( )
6. groundbreaking ( )
7. combat ( )
8. one and done ( )
9. cochlear implants ( )
10. obstacles ( )

❏ 選択肢 ❏

A. To fight or overcome
B. Amazed or surprised
C. A young child aged 2 to 4
D. Completed in one try
E. Devices that help deaf people hear
F. To get something back
G. Treating diseases by changing genes
H. Challenges or difficulties
I. New and innovative
J. Unable to hear

Task 3 (Viewing & Scanning: Answer the Multiple-Choice Questions)

動画を視聴し、次の質問の答えを、A~Dより選びましょう。

1. What type of treatment did Opal Sandy receive to restore her hearing?
   A) Gene therapy
   B) Cochlear implant surgery
   C) Antibiotic treatment
   D) Auditory training therapy

2. How long after the surgery did Opal's parents notice improvements in her hearing?
   A) Immediately
   B) 6 weeks
   C) 12 weeks
   D) 24 weeks

3. What was a significant observation made by Opal's parents about her hearing?
   A) She could hear loud noises only.   B) She responded to very soft sounds.
   C) She developed better speech.   D) She could hear only high-frequency sounds.

4. Who described the effects of the treatment as 'mind-blowing'?
   A) Opal's mother
   B) Opal's father
   C) The surgeon
   D) Both parents

Task 4 (Dictation) 🎧13

動画を音声に注意して視聴し、下線の部分にチャンク（英語数語）を書き込みましょう。

Banging on blocks and playing the flute, Opal Sandy looks like an [1]........................ ....

It would be hard to tell she was born deaf—and unable to hear just months earlier.

(Jo Sandy, Mother)
She's the first patient in England to regain her hearing [2]..................................... 5
....

"That was [3].., and we heard the phrase 'near-normal hearing', and she was [4]..."

(James Sandy, Father)
"Yeah, they played us the sounds that she was turning to and we were quite mind- 10 blown by [5]......................................, how quiet it was. They were sounds that I think in day-to-day life you might not even notice yourself, sort of thing."

Opal received treatment as part of a groundbreaking global gene therapy trial, which doctors say can combat various genetic conditions [6]..................................... .... in children. 15

(Manohar Bance, Surgeon)
"We can start to use gene therapy in young children, restore hearing for a variety of different kinds of genetic hearing loss, and then have a more 'one and done' type approach where we actually restore the hearing, we don't have to have cochlear implants and other technologies that [7]..."

Opal's parents [8]... as mind-blowing.

(Jo Sandy)
"I think we've been given a really unique opportunity [9].. that any harm or adverse effects were likely to come to her and I think a lot of parents, [10]... their children face, to be given an opportunity to potentially make obstacles easier for her to overcome was a risk definitely worth taking."

Task 5 (Reading: Answer the Questions in Japanese)

Task 4 で完成した英語ニュースを読んで、次の質問に日本語で答えましょう。Words & Phrases も参考にしましょう。

> **Words & Phrases**
> **banging on blocks** ブロックを叩く／ **day-to-day life** 日常生活／ **groundbreaking** 画期的な／ **restore** 回復する、回復させる／ **adverse effects** 副作用

1. ニュースの冒頭で、Opal Sandy のどのような様子が描写されていますか。

2. Opal Sandy は、イギリスでどのようなことをした、最初の患者となりましたか。

3. 遺伝子治療の利点として、医師が述べている点は何ですか。

4. Opal Sandy の治療後、彼女の両親が驚いたことは何ですか。

5. Opal Sandy の両親が、今回の治療を受ける価値があると考えた理由は何ですか。

Task 6 (Summary)

かっこに英語1語を入れて、動画ニュースの内容をまとめましょう。なお、ヒントになるよう、最初の文字を指定しています。

Words & Phrases
intervention 介入、治療処置／eliminate 取り除く

A toddler named Opal Sandy, born [d　　　　] due to genetic conditions, has regained her hearing through a groundbreaking gene therapy in England. She is the first [p　　　　] in the country to achieve near-normal hearing without the use of cochlear [i　　　　]. Doctors view this medical innovation as a potential treatment for various genetic causes of hearing [l　　　　] in children. The surgical intervention offers a "one and [d　　　　]" approach, eliminating the need for ongoing treatments. Opal's parents are thrilled with the therapeutic outcome and believe the risk assessment was worth the potential benefits.

Task 7 (Writing & Speaking)

本文や Task 6 を参考にして、遺伝子治療について、自由に英語で数行書いてみましょう。また、ペアで発表をしてみましょう。

Unit 7: This AI 'Turtle' Soup Is Helping the Endangered Species

YouTube

Task 1 (Guessing & Skimming)

動画を視聴する前に、写真と Key Words を見て内容を推測してみましょう。推測した内容をペアで話し合ってみましょう。

Key Words

1. delicacy
2. no trace of
3. recreate
4. endangered species
5. meat alternatives
6. peruse
7. plant-derived ingredients
8. impact
9. controversial
10. exploitation

Task 2 (Matching)

Key Words の内容を表している英語を下の選択肢 A〜J より選び、Key Words の意味を確認しましょう。

1. delicacy (　)
2. no trace of (　)
3. recreate (　)
4. endangered species (　)
5. meat alternatives (　)
6. peruse (　)
7. plant-derived ingredients (　)
8. impact (　)
9. controversial (　)
10. exploitation (　)

❏ 選択肢 ❏

A. Food components that come from plants
B. Completely absent; not even a little bit
C. A type of organism at serious risk of extinction
D. A strong effect or influence
E. Make a copy of something; make something exist again
F. A rare, delicious, and often expensive food
G. Using someone or something unfairly for personal gain
H. Causing a lot of disagreement or argument
I. To examine something carefully
J. Plant-based foods that mimic the taste and texture of meat

Task 3 (Viewing & Scanning: Answer the Multiple-Choice Questions)

動画を視聴し、次の質問の答えを、A〜D より選びましょう。

1. What role does artificial intelligence play in the company's food production process?
   A) It analyzes animal-based food structures at the molecular level.
   B) It is used to design new kitchen equipment.
   C) It handles marketing and sales of the products.
   D) It is used for financial analysis only.

2. What is one of the main goals of the company using AI to recreate dishes like turtle soup?
   A) To increase company profits by cutting costs
   B) To expand their product line into cosmetics
   C) To raise awareness about endangered species
   D) To reduce cooking time for all their products

3. What does the AI platform 'Giuseppe' do with the data it collects on animal-based foods?
   A) Predicts future food trends
   B) Replicates the food using only plant-based ingredients
   C) Sells the data to other companies
   D) Creates packaging for food products

4. Why are the AI-made turtle meat and soup not available for sale currently?
   A) Due to legal restrictions on sea turtle products
   B) The company is still perfecting the recipe.
   C) They are focusing on educational programs instead.
   D) It is available but only in select locations.

Task 4 (Dictation)

動画を音声に注意して視聴し、下線の部分にチャンク（英語数語）を書き込みましょう。

This dish tastes just like turtle soup, a delicacy in Chile . . . but there is no trace of the endangered green sea turtle [1]_____.

A plant-based food products company in Chile recreated [2]_____ using artificial intelligence. Their aim is to help raise awareness [3]_____ _____ while providing AI-enhanced meat alternatives.

Here in the NotCo lab in Santiago, Culinary Sciences Chief Bernardo Moltedo peruses the shelves that house a variety of plant-derived ingredients.

"We wanted to make an impact through artificial intelligence. We know that the use of AI is controversial, and we have been working on it for several years."

The company creates foods such as hamburgers, milk, mayonnaise and ice cream that [4] .... of traditional animal-based ingredients.

They say their AI platform Giuseppe [5] .... of an animal-based food at its molecular level . . . and then [6] .... only plants-based ingredients.

"We see it as a challenge and a very capable tool for transmitting what we want to do quickly and solving industry and environmental issues."

Moltedo says the effort isn't necessarily about dealing with all endangered species, but about being able to generate a [7] ....

"We can bring this to Latin America and give them a better alternative food through a plant-based approach."

The AI-made turtle meat and the soup [8] .... at the moment. But the company plans on holding a virtual class to teach people [9] .... The exploitation of sea turtles [10] .... and they are on the International Union for the Conservation of Nature's red list of threatened species.

Task 5 (Reading: Answer the Questions in Japanese)

Task 4 で完成した英語ニュースを読んで、次の質問に日本語で答えましょう。Words & Phrases も参考にしましょう。

> **Words & Phrases**
>
> **artificial intelligence** 人工知能、**AI / AI-enhanced** AI を活用した／**house** 収める、収納する／**Giuseppe** チリの食品テクノロジー企業 NotCo 社によって開発された人工知能システムの名前／**at its molecular level** 分子レベルで／**transmit** 伝える、残す／**red list of threatened species** 絶滅危惧種リスト

1. チリの植物性食品会社が人工知能を使って作った料理の味や食材について、どのように言っていますか。

   ....

   ....

2. チリの食品会社が、AI を活用してこのような料理を作る目的は何ですか。

   ....

   ....

3. ウミガメスープ以外に、NotCo 社が開発している動物性食品の代替品をいくつかあげてみましょう。

   ....

   ....

4. AI プラットフォーム「Giuseppe」は、どのようなことに挑戦していますか。

   ....

   ....

5. NotCo 社が開発したウミガメスープの代替品は、現時点でどのように考えられ、どのように活用される予定と言っていますか。

   ....

   ....

Task 6 (Summary)

かっこに英語1語を入れて、動画ニュースの内容をまとめましょう。なお、ヒントになるよう、最初の文字を指定しています。

Words & Phrases
innovation 革新、新機軸／consumption 食べること、摂取

A Chilean company has recreated a traditional Chilean [d   ], turtle soup, without harming any [e   ] species. Using artificial intelligence, their AI platform Giuseppe conducts molecular analysis of animal-based foods and replicates them with plant-derived [i   ]. This innovation aims to provide meat alternatives that raise [a   ] about environmental issues and generate a positive cultural impact. While the AI-made turtle soup isn't for sale yet, the company plans to hold virtual classes to teach people how to prepare it, supporting conservation efforts by discouraging the consumption of [t   ] species.

Task 7 (Writing & Speaking)

本文やTask 6を参考にして、絶滅危惧種の料理や絶滅危惧の動物について、自由に英語で数行書いてみましょう。また、ペアで発表をしてみましょう。

....

....

....

....

....

Unit 8　EU: Ocean Temperature Hit Record High in February

YouTube

Task 1　(Guessing & Skimming)

動画を視聴する前に、写真と Key Words を見て内容を推測してみましょう。推測した内容をペアで話し合ってみましょう。

Key Words

1. ocean　　　2. starting milestone　　3. record　　4. climate change
5. El Niño　　6. ecosystem　　　　　　7. coral　　　8. marine
9. CS3　　　　10. Antarctic

....
....
....
....

Task 2 (Matching)

Key Wordsの内容を表している英語を下の選択肢A~Jより選び、Key Wordsの意味を確認しましょう。

1. ocean (　)
2. starting milestone (　)
3. record (　)
4. climate change (　)
5. El Niño (　)
6. ecosystem (　)
7. coral (　)
8. marine (　)
9. CS3 (　)
10. Antarctic (　)

❏ 選択肢 ❏

A. The highest or lowest level achieved
B. A surprising or unexpected significant event or achievement
C. The Earth's southernmost continent, covered in ice
D. Long-term alterations in average weather patterns
E. A marine animal that lives in colonies and forms reefs
F. A climate pattern characterized by warm ocean waters in the Pacific
G. Copernicus Climate Change Service: The European Union's Earth observation program that monitors climate change
H. A biological community interacting with its environment
I. Relating to the sea or sea life
J. A large body of salt water that covers approximately 70% of the earth's surface

Task 3 (Viewing & Scanning: Answer the Multiple-Choice Questions)

動画を視聴し、次の質問の答えを、A~Dより選びましょう。

1. What did the ocean temperatures reach in February according to the EU's Copernicus Climate Change Service?
   A) A new low record
   B) A normal temperature
   C) The highest temperature ever recorded
   D) A slightly above average temperature

2. What natural phenomenon contributed to the extra heat in the ocean?
   A) El Niño   B) Global warming
   C) La Nina   D) Ocean currents

3. What environmental issue did marine scientists warn about recently?
   A) Oil pollution   B) Coral bleaching
   C) Overfishing   D) Plastic pollution

4. What happens to corals when they bleach?
   A) They grow faster.   B) They expel algae and turn pale.
   C) They absorb more sunlight. D) They sink to the ocean floor.

Task 4 (Dictation) 17

動画を音声に注意して視聴し、下線の部分にチャンク（英語数語）を書き込みましょう。

Ocean temperatures hit their highest all-time record in February—a startling milestone that saw the surface of the world's seas hit 69.9 degrees Fahrenheit [1] _____.

That's according to the EU's Copernicus Climate Change Service, or CS3, on Thursday. They say the new record broke a previous average of almost 69.8 degrees in the Northern hemisphere's summer, last August, in a dataset that goes back to 1979. This last month was also the [2] _____, the ninth consecutive month to set their own monthly record.

An El Niño climate pattern this year, fueled by [3] _____ in the Eastern Pacific is driving extra heat.

However, Carlo Buontempo, director of the CS3 says human-caused climate change is still largely to blame.

"So there are a number of co-causes, but fundamentally—and these are fluctuations, so you have, as for El Niño, positive phases and negative phases. So on the long term average, they typically average to zero—but [4]... adding up because we keep pumping greenhouse gases in the atmosphere, and so this fundamentally makes new temperature records more [5].."

This week, marine scientists warned of a likely fourth global mass coral bleaching event in the Southern Hemisphere, potentially [6]... due to warming waters.

Corals bleach under heat stress and will expel the helpful algae that live in their tissues, [7]... a pale skeleton, which makes them vulnerable to [8]..., and many die. That can lead to the collapse of reef ecosystems, leaving coastlines vulnerable and fisheries depleted.

While the global sea surface temperature record excludes [9].., conditions there are also concerning. Antarctic sea ice hit its third lowest extent on record in February, 28% below average. The CS3 said El Niño [10] .... in the equatorial Pacific, but the air temperatures over the oceans remain at an unusually high level.

Task 5 (Reading: Answer the Questions in Japanese)

Task 4 で完成した英語ニュースを読んで、次の質問に日本語で答えましょう。Words & Phrases も参考にしましょう。

Words & Phrases

all-time record 史上最高記録／**Fahrenheit** 華氏度（華氏 69.6 度は摂氏 21.06 度にあたる）／**hemisphere** 半球／**expel** 排出する／**algae** 藻類／**deplete** 激減させる／**exclude** ～を除く

1. CS3 によると、今回の記録的な海水温はどの期間のデータセットに基づいていますか。

2. Carlo Buontempo が述べた、気候変動の主な原因は何ですか。

3. サンゴが白化する原因は何ですか。

4. サンゴの白化により、どのような影響が考えられますか。

5. 南極の海氷が、2 月に記録した状況はどうでしたか。

Task 6 (Summary)

かっこに英語１語を入れて、動画ニュースの内容をまとめましょう。なお、ヒントになるよう、最初の文字を指定しています。

Words & Phrases
trigger 引き起こす、〜のきっかけとなる

Ocean temperatures hit their highest [r   ] in February, averaging 69.9 degrees Fahrenheit, according to the EU's Copernicus Climate Change Service (CS3). This unprecedented rise is attributed to human-induced [c   ] change and an ongoing El Niño event, leading to extra heat in the oceans. [M   ] scientists warn that warming waters may trigger a fourth global mass [c   ] bleaching event, potentially the worst in history, threatening vital [e   ]. Additionally, Antarctic sea ice reached its third lowest extent on record, intensifying concerns about the global climate crisis.

Task 7 (Writing & Speaking)

本文や Task 6 を参考にして、エルニーニョや台風など自然現象について、自由に英語で数行書いてみましょう。また、ペアで発表をしてみましょう。

....
....
....
....
....

This Florida Shark Prof Wants Girls to Dive into Science

YouTube

 (Guessing & Skimming)

動画を視聴する前に、写真と Key Words を見て内容を推測してみましょう。推測した内容をペアで話し合ってみましょう。

Key Words

1. hold clues
2. underwater ecosystem
3. conservation
4. weekly expedition
5. shark habitats
6. function
7. human-caused alterations
8. get one's foot in the door
9. land in a lab
10. geared towards

....
....
....

Task 2 (Matching)

Key Words の内容を表している英語を下の選択肢 A〜J より選び、Key Words の意味を確認しましょう。

1. hold clues (　)
2. underwater ecosystem (　)
3. conservation (　)
4. weekly expedition (　)
5. shark habitats (　)
6. function (　)
7. human-caused alterations (　)
8. get one's foot in the door (　)
9. land in a lab (　)
10. geared towards (　)

❏ 選択肢 ❏

A. A community of plants, animals, and tiny organisms living and interacting in water
B. To get a job to work in a laboratory
C. Natural areas where sharks live, including specific ocean conditions like temperature and depth.
D. A regular weekly trip for exploration or research
E. Environmental changes due to human actions like pollution or deforestation
F. To operate or work in a proper or particular way
G. To have information that helps solve a question or mystery
H. Made for a specific purpose or group
I. To start working in a field, often through an entry-level role
J. Protecting and preserving nature, resources, and wildlife

Task 3 (Viewing & Scanning: Answer the Multiple-Choice Questions)

動画を視聴し、次の質問の答えを、A〜D より選びましょう。

1. What is the goal of the weekly expeditions led by Professor Macdonald?
   A) To understand shark habitats better
   B) To study the habits of dolphins
   C) To clean up the underwater ecosystem
   D) To map the ocean floor

2. Why did Haley Aker face difficulties in pursuing her interest in sharks?
   A) She lived far from the ocean.
   B) She lacked the necessary education.
   C) She was not interested in volunteering.
   D) Labs were selecting males as volunteers.

3. What kind of letters does Professor Macdonald receive from young girls?
   A) Letters asking how to become like her
   B) Letters asking how to apply to shark labs
   C) Letters asking for internships
   D) Letters asking for funding

4. What age group are the trips organized by Professor Macdonald specifically aimed at?
   A) Elementary school girls
   B) Middle school girls
   C) High school girls
   D) College students

Task 4 (Dictation)

動画を音声に注意して視聴し、下線の部分にチャンク（英語数語）を書き込みましょう。

This shark could hold clues to the state of the underwater ecosystem in southern Florida's Biscayne Bay. Professor Catherine Macdonald runs the University of Miami's [1]_____. The goal of weekly expeditions like this is [2]_____.

"The samples that we took today help us answer questions about [3]_____ now. But they will also help us answer questions about how it's changing in the face of the human-caused alterations that we know are coming in the future."

Macdonald has another passion, too: getting women and girls [4]_____. Macdonald's newest intern, undergraduate student Haley Aker, says it [5]_____ sailing trying to pursue her love of sharks.

52   Unit 9

"I have been obsessed with them since I was a little kid. And I've always lived near the water. I applied to numerous shark labs and tried to get my foot in the door. But it seemed that they only were selecting [6]... and their helpers, and they just didn't—I believe that they just didn't think that I was smart enough or could do it, you know, [7]... . And, finally being able to come here and be given this opportunity to work with sharks and, you know, work on my dream has been awesome. And I love that I'm finally able to, like, prove myself."

Macdonald: "I get letters from young girls who are excited about shark science, sometimes just asking scientific questions, sometimes asking how they can [8]... . And, I think for my whole lab, answering those questions, responding to those girls is one of the things that we find really deeply rewarding."

Macdonald hopes some of those letter writers might eventually land in a lab like hers.

"We run trips that are intentionally geared [9]..., which studies show is an age at which, many girls sort of start to think that maybe science isn't for them. And the chance to watch them connect with my undergraduate interns and my graduate students is really meaningful."

"When they ask me how I don't lose hope, because conservation is [10]..., but often a sad and challenging one. How, where would I get the nerve to give up if they're not?"

Task 5 (Reading: Answer the Questions in Japanese)

Task 4 で完成した英語ニュースを読んで、次の質問に日本語で答えましょう。Words & Phrases も参考にしましょう。

Words & Phrases
undergraduate student 学部生／**apply to** 申し込む／**awesome** 素晴らしい／**deeply rewarding** 本当に深く報われる／**intentionally** 意図的に／**graduate student** 大学院生

1. ビスケーン湾でのサメの調査による「水中生態系の手がかり」とは、どのようなことを意味していますか。

    ....
    ....

2. Macdonald 教授が女性に科学への関心を持ってもらうため、行っているプログラムはどのようなものですか。

    ....
    ....

3. 学部生の Haley Aker が、Macdonald 教授の研究室のインターンになる前に、数々のサメの研究室に申し込んだ際、どのような経験をしましたか。

    ....
    ....

4. 学部生の Haley Aker は、Macdonald 教授の研究室のインターンになり、今どのような気持ちでいますか。

    ....
    ....

5. Macdonald 教授は、若い女性や少女たちからよく問い合わせの手紙を受け取りますが、その質問内容は主にどのようなことについてですか。

    ....
    ....

Task 6 (Summary)

かっこに英語1語を入れて、動画ニュースの内容をまとめましょう。なお、ヒントになるよう、最初の文字を指定しています。

Words & Phrases

feels empowered 研究者として自立していると感じている

Professor Catherine Macdonald leads weekly expeditions to study the [u   ] ecosystem and shark habitats in Biscayne Bay. These trips aim to gather samples that hold [c   ] about how this ecosystem is [f   ] and how human-caused alterations might affect it in the future. Macdonald is also passionate about conservation and encouraging young women to enter science. She organizes trips [g   ] towards middle school girls to inspire them to pursue careers in science. Her intern, Haley Aker, faced challenges in getting her [f   ] in the door but now feels empowered working in a lab dedicated to marine research.

Task 7 (Writing & Speaking)

本文やTask 6を参考にして、自分が関心がある職業、あるいは、将来就きたい職業について、自由に英語で数行書いてみましょう。また、ペアで発表をしてみましょう。

Unit 10 Pig-to-human Kidney Transplant Success May Offer Hope

YouTube

Task 1 (Guessing & Skimming)

動画を視聴する前に、写真と Key Words を見て内容を推測してみましょう。推測した内容をペアで話し合ってみましょう。

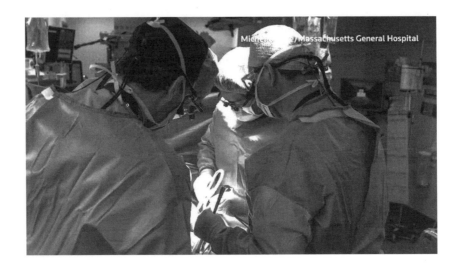

Key Words

1. breakthrough
2. end-stage renal disease
3. dialysis
4. genetically edited
5. recipient
6. compatibility
7. cadaveric kidney donation
8. insufficient to fill that need
9. xenotransplantation
10. life support

Task 2 (Matching)

Key Words の内容を表している英語を下の選択肢 A~J より選び、Key Words の意味を確認しましょう。

1. breakthrough (　　)
2. end-stage renal disease (　　)
3. dialysis (　　)
4. genetically edited (　　)
5. recipient (　　)
6. compatibility (　　)
7. cadaveric kidney donation (　　)
8. insufficient to fill that need (　　)
9. xenotransplantation (　　)
10. life support (　　)

❏ 選択肢 ❏

A. The process of transplanting organs or tissues between different species
B. Modified at the genetic level to change certain traits or characteristics
C. The final phase of chronic kidney disease where the kidneys can no longer function on their own
D. A medical treatment that filters and purifies the blood using a machine when the kidneys are no longer able to perform this function
E. The person receiving a transplant
F. It refers to how well the transplanted organ matches and functions with the recipient's body, minimizing the risk of rejection
G. A significant development or discovery that advances understanding or capability
H. Obtaining a kidney from a deceased donor for transplantation
I. Medical equipment that keeps a person alive when their vital organs are not functioning properly
J. Not enough to meet the demand or requirement

Task 3 (Viewing & Scanning: Answer the Multiple-Choice Questions)

動画を視聴し、次の質問の答えを、A~D より選びましょう。

1. What organ was transplanted from a pig to a human in the described surgery?
   A) Heart
   B) Liver
   C) Kidney
   D) Lung

2. What is the main purpose of genetically editing the pig's organs before transplantation?
   A) To increase the size of the organs   B) To remove harmful genes
   C) To change the organ's color   D) To make the organs glow in the dark

3. What was the patient's condition before receiving the pig kidney transplant?
   A) Diabetic neuropathy   B) Liver cirrhosis
   C) Heart failure   D) End-stage renal disease

4. What is the expected minimum duration that the transplanted pig kidney is hoped to last in the human patient?
   A) 6 months   B) 1 year
   C) 2 years   D) 5 years

Task 4 (Dictation)

動画を音声に注意して視聴し、下線の部分にチャンク（英語数語）を書き込みましょう。

Dr. Tatsuo Kawai: "It was truly the most beautiful kidney I have ever seen."

Transplant surgeon Dr. Tatsuo Kawai and his team are hailing what they call a major breakthrough, after what they say is the first ever successful transplant of [1] .... into a live human patient.
Kawai described the moment after the kidney was hooked up to the 62-year-old man who [2] ....

"Upon restoration of blood flow into the kidneys, the kidney pinked up immediately and started to make urine. When we saw the first urine output everyone in the operating room burst in applause."

The four-hour surgery was performed on March 16 at the Massachusetts General Hospital in Boston.
The hospital said [3] .... and set to be discharged soon.

58　Unit 10

He had received a human kidney transplant at the same hospital in 2018, after seven years on dialysis.

But the organ failed five years later, putting him back on dialysis. His new kidney was provided by biotech company eGenesis, from a pig with about the same sized organs that had been genetically edited to [4] .... to a human recipient. Certain human genes were also added to improve compatibility. And some viruses inherent to pigs with the [5] .... were inactivated.

The renal experts are hoping the transplanted organ will [6] .... eGenesis CEO Dr. Mike Curtis sees this surgery as a milestone that could [7] .... for the queue of some 90,000 Americans waiting for donor kidneys.

"Many of those patients will spend their final days on dialysis. That's just the patients on the transplant waiting list. If we look more broadly at the patients with kidney failure on dialysis, we're talking about hundreds of thousands of patients [8] .... a kidney transplant. And the reality is, with our current cadaveric kidney donation system, it's just insufficient to fill that need."

Researchers have been working for decades on the [9] .... for transplants, known as xenotransplantation, but [10] .... has been a stumbling block.

In 2021, NYU surgeons had successfully transplanted a genetically modified pig kidney into a braindead patient, whose family consented to the experiment shortly before life support was due to be switched off.

Task 5 (Reading: Answer the Questions in Japanese)

Task 4 で完成した英語ニュースを読んで、次の質問に日本語で答えましょう。Words & Phrases も参考にしましょう。

Words & Phrases

transplant surgeon　移植外科医／hail　称賛する／hooked up　つながれた／upon restoration　回復するとすぐに／urine　尿／be discharged　退院する／milestone　画期的な出来事／stumbling block　障害／braindead patient　脳死患者

---

1. 移植された腎臓は、すぐにどのような反応を示しましたか。

   ....
   ....

2. eGenesis 社が提供した豚の腎臓は、どのように遺伝的に編集されましたか。

   ....
   ....

3. この患者が以前受けた移植と、その後の彼の状況について説明してください。

   ....
   ....

4. 他の動物からの臓器の異種移植が成功した場合、どのようなことが期待されますか。

   ....
   ....

5. 他の動物から人間への異種移植の問題点として、これまでどのようなことが指摘されていましたか。

   ....
   ....

Task 6 (Summary)

かっこに英語１語を入れて、動画ニュースの内容をまとめましょう。なお、ヒントになるよう、最初の文字を指定しています。

Words & Phrases

reliant on ～に頼っている／**revolutionize** ～に一大進歩をもたらす

In a medical [b   ], surgeons at Massachusetts General Hospital performed the first successful [t   ] of a genetically modified pig kidney into a live human patient with end-stage renal disease. The kidney, provided by biotech company eGenesis, was engineered to improve compatibility by [r   ] harmful genes and adding human ones, while viruses [i   ] to pigs were inactivated. The patient, previously reliant on [d   ], is recovering well. This advancement in xenotransplantation offers hope to the 90,000 Americans awaiting donor kidneys and could revolutionize organ transplantation.

Task 7 (Writing & Speaking)

本文や Task 6 を参考にして、医学の進歩や自分が受けた手術などについて、自由に英語で数行書いてみましょう。また、ペアで発表をしてみましょう。

....
....
....
....
....

Unit 11: Researchers Make Medical Tests from Used Chewing Gum

YouTube

Task 1 (Guessing & Skimming)

動画を視聴する前に、写真と Key Words を見て内容を推測してみましょう。推測した内容をペアで話し合ってみましょう。

Key Words

1. single-use
2. lateral flow tests (LFTs)
3. recycled materials
4. virgin plastic
5. carbon footprint
6. prototype
7. contamination
8. incinerate
9. embark on
10. sustainable

Task 2 (Matching)

Key Words の内容を表している英語を下の選択肢 A～J より選び、Key Words の意味を確認しましょう。

1. single-use (　　)
2. lateral flow tests (LFTs) (　　)
3. recycled materials (　　)
4. virgin plastic (　　)
5. carbon footprint (　　)
6. prototype (　　)
7. contamination (　　)
8. incinerate (　　)
9. embark on (　　)
10. sustainable (　　)

❑ 選択肢 ❑

A. To begin or start a new project, venture, or journey
B. The total amount of greenhouse gases, particularly carbon dioxide, emitted directly or indirectly by an individual, organization, or product
C. To burn waste materials to reduce their volume and potentially generate energy
D. The presence of harmful or unwanted substances that can cause pollution or adverse effects
E. Products designed to be used once and then discarded
F. An early model or version of a product that is developed for testing and evaluation purposes
G. Newly manufactured plastic that has not been previously used or processed
H. Able to be maintained or continued over time without causing harm, especially to the environment
I. Materials that have been processed to be reused or transformed into new products, reducing waste and environmental impact
J. Diagnostic devices used to confirm the presence or absence of a target substance

Task 3 (Viewing & Scanning: Answer the Multiple-Choice Questions)

動画を視聴し、次の質問の答えを、A～D より選びましょう。

1. What is the main reason for using recycled materials in medical tests?
   A. Lower costs
   B. Increased efficiency
   C. Reducing environmental impact
   D. Improving test accuracy

2. What type of medical tests are made with used chewing gum?
   A. Lateral flow tests   B. MRI scans
   C. Blood tests   D. X-rays

3. Which university is involved in the research for using recycled materials in medical tests?
   A. University of Edinburgh   B. Oxford University
   C. University of Glasgow   D. Heriot-Watt University

4. What is a major challenge in recycling plastics used in medical testing?
   A. Finding enough materials   B. Sorting and contamination issues
   C. Lack of technology   D. High costs

Task 4 (Dictation) 23

動画を音声に注意して視聴し、下線の部分にチャンク（英語数語）を書き込みましょう。

Some of these single-use medical tests—called lateral flow tests—were created with discarded chewing gum.

Researchers in Scotland are turning to the chewy treat and other recycled materials in hopes of making a dent in a huge [1].. .

Every year, billions of lateral flow tests—or LFTs— [2]... .... to test for illnesses, like COVID and malaria, and also for conditions, like pregnancy.
Not only are they simply thrown away [3]..., but they're also made of virgin plastic material.

(Maiwenn Kersaudy-Kerhoas, Heriot-Watt University)
"What we're asking here is, do they have to be made out of virgin plastic? Could we remove the carbon footprint of the virgin plastic production in this specific use case?"

[4] .... tons (16,000 tonnes) of plastics are produced for rapid-LFT testing every year, with an average test containing up to 15 grams of single-use virgin plastic. That's according to Maiwenn Kersaudy-Kerhoas, a researcher and professor at Scotland's Heriot-Watt University. [5] .... Great Central Plastics, her research team has produced five prototype devices made from a range of recycled materials, including chewing gum.

"What we're hoping is that through the use of these cassettes, we can [6] .... the regulations, on the economics, on the customer acceptance of these new materials and ultimately save 30 to 50% of the carbon footprint of the virgin material production."

Currently, very few plastics used in medical testing are recycled because of issues due to [7] .... So, most are incinerated or sent to a landfill.

Alice Street, a professor at the University of Edinburgh, says it's an urgent issue to address.
"Really this is the challenge of modern healthcare, that in order to save lives and improve health, we are producing huge numbers of single use plastic devices. But those same devices are also [8] .... of plastic pollution globally . . ." "We need not only healthcare systems that will contribute to growth on the health, we also need health care systems that are themselves healthy."

Kiron Phillips of Great Central Plastics says the team has the machinery and knowledge to shift the industry's mindset. "There are many professionals within the UK that would be able to [9] .... and move into a more sustainable option on products like this."

[10] .... , the team has also developed LFTs using four other sustainably derived plastics such as old fridge parts. They now have approval to test their prototypes to make sure they function just as well as existing LFTs.

Task 5 (Reading: Answer the Questions in Japanese)

Task 4 で完成した英語ニュースを読んで、次の質問に日本語で答えましょう。Words & Phrases も参考にしましょう。

Words & Phrases

make a dent 歯止めをかける／**Heriot-Watt University**（ヘリオット・ワット大学：スコットランドの首都エジンバラ市に本部を置くイギリスの公立大学）／**ton** トン（アメリカで使用される単位で 1 ton は約 907 キログラム／**tonne**（メトリックトンとも言う。イギリスや日本で使用される単位で、1 tonne は 1,000 キログラム）／**Great Central Plastics**（グレート・セントラル・プラスチックス：プラスチック射出成形メーカー）／**regulation**（法的）規制／**landfill** 埋め立て式ごみ処理／**Kiron Phillips of Great Central Plastics** イギリス、ノーサンプトンシャーにあるプラスチック射出成形会社／**mindset** 意識／**sustainable** 持続可能な

1. 使用済みのガムをリサイクルすることの、主な目的は何ですか。

   ....
   ....

2. 毎年数十億個も作られる迅速検査キットは、たとえばどのような検査に使われていますか。

   ....
   ....

3. 一連のリサイクル材料から作られた 5 つのプロトタイプを使用することで、どのくらいバージン素材の生産に関連する炭素排出量を削減することが期待されていますか。

   ....
   ....

4. 現在、医療検査に使用されるプラスチックのほとんどがリサイクルされず、どのように処理されていますか。

   ....
   ....

5. Great Central Plastics のチームは、承認を得て、現在どのようなテストを行っていますか。

   ....
   ....

Task 6 (Summary)

かっこに英語1語を入れて、動画ニュースの内容をまとめましょう。なお、ヒントになるよう、最初の文字を指定しています。

> Researchers at Heriot-Watt University in Scotland are tackling plastic [p   ] by developing innovative lateral flow tests (LFTs) made from recycled [m   ], including discarded chewing gum and old fridge parts. In collaboration with Great Central Plastics, they have produced [p   ] aiming to reduce the environmental impact of single-use medical devices in healthcare. Currently, billions of LFTs made from virgin plastic are discarded annually, [c   ] to significant waste. This recycling initiative could cut the carbon [f   ] of these tests by up to 50%, promoting greater sustainability in the industry.

Task 7 (Writing & Speaking)

本文やTask 6を参考にして、中古品の再利用について、自由に英語で数行書いてみましょう。また、ペアで発表をしてみましょう。

....

....

....

....

....

Unit 12 Seaweed Microrobots Could One Day Treat Cancer, Researcher Says

Task 1 (Guessing & Skimming)

動画を視聴する前に、写真と Key Words を見て内容を推測してみましょう。推測した内容をペアで話し合ってみましょう。

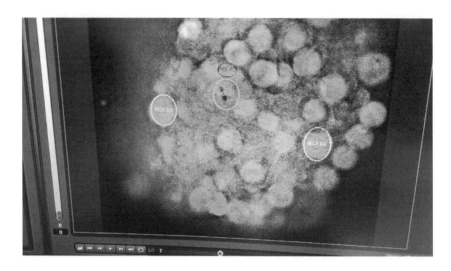

Key Words

1. stimulate
2. in a targeted manner
3. potential
4. synthetic conditions
5. manufacture
6. repair damaged tissue
7. width
8. therapeutics
9. clusters
10. underway

....
....
....
....

Task 2 (Matching)

Key Words の内容を表している英語を下の選択肢 A~J より選び、Key Words の意味を確認しましょう。

1. stimulate (　)
2. in a targeted manner (　)
3. potential (　)
4. synthetic conditions (　)
5. manufacture (　)
6. repair damaged tissue (　)
7. width (　)
8. therapeutics (　)
9. clusters (　)
10. underway (　)

❏ 選択肢 ❏

A. Artificial or laboratory-created environments
B. In a way that is directed or focused on a specific area or purpose
C. Medicines or treatments used to cure or alleviate diseases and medical conditions
D. The capacity or possibility for something to develop or succeed in the future
E. The measurement or extent of something from side to side
F. Something is happening now or in progress
G. To produce or create something on a large scale, typically in a systematic or industrial way
H. To activate, energize, or encourage activity or growth
I. Groups or collections of similar items or organisms located close together
J. To restore injured or compromised biological tissue to a healthy state

Task 3 (Viewing & Scanning: Answer the Multiple-Choice Questions)

動画を視聴し、次の質問の答えを、A~D より選びましょう。

1. What is a unique feature of the microrobots mentioned in the article?
   A. They can change their color to blend in with cells.
   B. They are designed to replicate human emotions.
   C. They can only be used outside of the human body.
   D. They can stimulate individual cells in a targeted manner.

2. According to researchers at the Technical University of Munich, what potential use might these microrobots have?
   A. They could serve as micro-cameras to record cellular activities.
   B. They might help create artificial organs.
   C. They could offer new treatment methods for cancer and other diseases.
   D. They might be used for space exploration in the future.

3. What materials are used to make these microrobots?
   A. Seaweed and gold nanoparticles
   B. Plastic and silicone
   C. Metal and glass
   D. Gel and silicon

4. How can the microrobots be controlled within cell clusters?
   A. Through voice commands
   B. By using a wireless joystick
   C. With a laser to heat certain areas of the robot
   D. By changing the color of the surrounding cells

Task 4 (Dictation) 25

動画を音声に注意して視聴し、下線の部分にチャンク（英語数語）を書き込みましょう。

These little green dots are microrobots. They can navigate in a cell network and [1] _____ in a targeted manner.

Researchers at the Technical University of Munich—or TUM—say the microrobot is the first of its kind . . . and has the [2] _____ for patients battling [3] _____.

Berna Ozkale Edelmann is the lead researcher at TUM.
"We are using these microrobots to build tissues under synthetic conditions. And the [4] _____ is to—in the future—then repair damaged

tissue or organs at a really patient's basis. So if I can, sort of like, you know, many manufacturing cars in a robotic factory."

The tiny robots are [5] .... and the team has found a way to produce millions of them in just minutes. They are about half the width of a human hair—or [6] .... human cells. They are soft like human cells, too, and can be controlled wirelessly.

Philipp Harder is a PhD student [7] .... "We have gold nanoparticles inside the robots. And with a laser, which we can see here, [8] .... of the robot. I'll let the video run for a moment. Then, when we point the laser [9] ...., we can see that it starts to move. And so, we can then move it within the cell clusters and move it to other locations and then look at several cells in different ways."

Ozkale Edelmann said the microrobots aren't ready [10] .... but that the technology is supporting research already underway. "The more we find out about these cells, the more, the better we can actually design therapeutics."

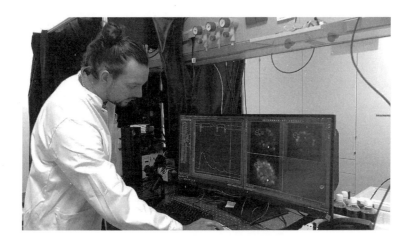

Task 5 (Reading: Answer the Questions in Japanese)

Task 4 で完成した英語ニュースを読んで、次の質問に日本語で答えましょう。Words & Phrases も参考にしましょう。

> **Words & Phrases**
> **cell network** 細胞ネットワーク／**Munich** ミュンヘン（ドイツのバイエルン州の州都）／**tissue** （細胞）組織／**nanoparticle** ナノ粒子（ナノメートルレベルの微細加工技術による粒子）／**design therapeutics** 治療法を設計する

1. 最初に、マイクロロボットは細胞ネットワーク内でどのようなことができると述べていますか。

   ....

   ....

2. このマイクロロボットは、どのような潜在的可能性を秘めていると言っていますか。

   ....

   ....

3. マイクロロボットの大きさは、どのくらいだと言っていますか。

   ....

   ....

4. マイクロロボットは、どのようにして移動させますか。

   ....

   ....

5. マイクロロボットは、がん患者にすぐに役立つわけではないと述べられていますが、現在はどのようなことに貢献していますか。

   ....

   ....

Task 6 (Summary)

かっこに英語1語を入れて、動画ニュースの内容をまとめましょう。なお、ヒントになるよう、最初の文字を指定しています。

Words & Phrases
therapeutic 治療の、治療上の

Researchers at the Technical University of Munich (TUM) have developed [m   ] made from seaweed that can navigate within cell networks and [s   ] individual cells in a targeted manner. These tiny robots, about half the [w   ] of a human hair, contain gold nanoparticles and can be controlled wirelessly using lasers. The [p   ] applications include building tissues under synthetic conditions to repair damaged tissue or organs, much like [m   ] cars in a robotic factory. While not yet ready for clinical use, this innovation advances research toward future therapeutic methods.

Task 7 (Writing & Speaking)

本文や Task 6 を参考にして、日常生活で AI が活躍していることについて、自由に英語で数行書いてみましょう。また、ペアで発表をしてみましょう。

....

....

....

....

....

Unit 13 Brazil Braces for Worst Coral Bleaching Ever

YouTube

Task 1 (Guessing & Skimming)

動画を視聴する前に、写真と Key Words を見て内容を推測してみましょう。推測した内容をペアで話し合ってみましょう。

Key Words
1. coral bleaching
2. marine reserve
3. metabolism
4. intensify
5. mass bleaching event
6. swath
7. tourism revenue
8. economic alternative
9. microalgae
10. resilient

Task 2 (Matching)

Key Words の内容を表している英語を下の選択肢 A~J より選び、Key Words の意味を確認しましょう。

1. coral bleaching (　　)
2. marine reserve (　　)
3. metabolism (　　)
4. intensify (　　)
5. mass bleaching event (　　)
6. swath (　　)
7. tourism revenue (　　)
8. economic alternative (　　)
9. microalgae (　　)
10. resilient (　　)

❏ 選択肢 ❏

A. A major coral bleaching occurrence that affects large reef areas simultaneously, often due to extreme environmental stress
B. A broad strip or area, often describing a wide range in a specific context
C. To increase the strength, degree, or force of something
D. Tiny photosynthetic organisms crucial for aquatic ecosystems, contributing to primary production and serving as food for marine life
E. A process where corals lose their color and turn white due to environmental stressors like high temperatures and pollution
F. Able to recover quickly from difficult conditions, such as illness, adversity, or misfortune
G. A strategy or an option for generating income, especially to replace traditional sources
H. Income generated from visitors traveling for leisure or business
I. The chemical processes in living organisms that convert food into energy
J. An ocean area protected for the conservation of marine life

Task 3 (Viewing & Scanning: Answer the Multiple-Choice Questions)

動画を視聴し、次の質問の答えを、A~D より選びましょう。

1: What is causing the current threat to the coral reefs in Brazil?
　A) Overfishing
　B) Pollution
　C) Coastal development
　D) Climate change

2: What is the main economic impact mentioned related to coral bleaching?
   A) Loss of biodiversity
   B) Decrease in tourism and fishing revenues
   C) Increase in scientific research funding
   D) Improvement in marine transportation

3: How does the local community depend on coral reefs, according to the article?
   A) For educational purposes
   B) For employment and income
   C) For leisure and recreation
   D) For artistic inspiration

4: What could help the corals recover from bleaching?
   A) Cooler water temperatures
   B) Reduction of fishing activities
   C) Increased water temperatures
   D) Removal of coral predators

Task 4 (Dictation)

動画を音声に注意して視聴し、下線の部分にチャンク（英語数語）を書き込みましょう。

Brazil is bracing for what may be its worst-ever coral bleaching event . . . as [1] _____ damage reefs in the country's largest marine reserve.

Pedro Pereira is a coordinator for the nonprofit Reef Conservation Project. "Coral reefs are very [2] _____, we've recorded temperatures of up to 33 degrees here in the region and any small temperature variation already affects the metabolism and causes [3] _____, which consequently causes, unfortunately, the death of a large number of these species."

Sea temperatures have smashed records in the last year as [4] _____ _____ the El Niño phenomenon that normally warms the globe every six or seven years. The world's corals are now suffering a fourth mass bleaching event in three decades. Some had hoped Brazil's reefs would be spared as they were during previous events.

But huge swaths of corals have turned bone white along Brazil's vast Atlantic coastline including the 75-mile marine park called Coral Coast. Nearly 100% of the corals in some parts of the marine park have been affected, and [5]........................... ...., a research director at the Coral Vivo Institute told Reuters.

And the issue is threatening the region's [6].. . "Tourism depends on coral reefs, fishing depends on coral reefs. So any alteration or change to this ecosystem will alter an entire production chain, including a community that depends on the resources of the sea for its survival."

Reef tourism generates an estimated $175 million each year for the relevant municipalities, according to the conservation charity Boticario Group Foundation. Thousands of people also work in small-scale fishing, virtually the only [7].............. .... in certain areas.

This year, [8]..., fish and prawns have all declined, according to a Coral Coast fisherman who spoke to Reuters. The reefs previously have only been hit by one deadly bleaching event in 2019-2020, which killed up to 50% of the region's distinct species of brain corals and 90% of its Branching Fire Coral.

Corals can recover [9]... for them to be repopulated by the microalgae that live in their tissue. Scientists say that whatever survives [10]...................................... what traits helped make it more resilient.

Task 5 (Reading: Answer the Questions in Japanese)

Task 4で完成した英語ニュースを読んで、次の質問に日本語で答えましょう。Words & Phrases も参考にしましょう。

Words & Phrases

brace 直面する、困難などに奮起する／nonprofit 非営利団体／Reef Conservation Project リーフ保護プロジェクト／species 種／be spared 命が助かる、生き残る／Coral Vivo Institute コーラルビボ研究所（主に南大西洋地域のサンゴ礁の研究と保護に取り組んでいる）／relevant municipalities 関連する市町村／prawn エビ／repopulate 再び住み着く／trait 特性

1. この記事によると、サンゴの白化現象が起こる原因は何ですか。

   ....

   ....

2. サンゴの白化によって、どのような経済的影響が発生していますか。

   ....

   ....

3. Coral Coast と呼ばれる海洋公園のサンゴの状態は、どのように報告されていますか。

   ....

   ....

4. サンゴが白化から回復するためには何が必要ですか。

   ....

   ....

5. 科学者たちはサンゴの将来について、どんな研究を提案していますか。

   ....

   ....

Task 6 (Summary)

かっこに英語1語を入れて、動画ニュースの内容をまとめましょう。なお、ヒントになるよう、最初の文字を指定しています。

Words & Phrases

pose （危険などを）引き起こす

Brazil is bracing for its worst-ever coral [b   ] event as extremely warm waters damage reefs in the country's largest marine [r   ]. The rise in sea temperatures, intensified by El Niño, has led to a fourth [m   ] bleaching event in three decades. Nearly 100% of corals in some areas have been affected, threatening the region's [t   ] revenue and fishing revenue. While corals can recover if waters cool and are [r   ] by microalgae, the current situation poses significant risks to local economies and ecosystems.

Task 7 (Writing & Speaking)

本文や Task 6 を参考にして、気候変動とその社会への影響について、自由に英語で数行書いてみましょう。また、ペアで発表をしてみましょう。

Unit 14: Researchers Uncover 'Phonetic Alphabet' of Sperm Whales

Task 1 (Guessing & Skimming)

動画を視聴する前に、写真と Key Words を見て内容を推測してみましょう。推測した内容をペアで話し合ってみましょう。

Key Words

1. codas
2. sophisticated
3. marine mammals
4. statistical analysis
5. vocalization
6. phonetic alphabet
7. pictographic systems
8. duration
9. behavioral data
10. social dynamics

Task 2 (Matching)

Key Words の内容を表している英語を下の選択肢A~Jより選び、Key Words の意味を確認しましょう。

1. codas (　　)
2. sophisticated (　　)
3. marine mammals (　　)
4. statistical analysis (　　)
5. vocalization (　　)
6. phonetic alphabet (　　)
7. pictographic systems (　　)
8. duration (　　)
9. behavioral data (　　)
10. social dynamics (　　)

❏ 選択肢 ❏

A. Specific sequences of clicking sounds used by whales for communication
B. The length of time that something lasts
C. Information that captures the actions and interactions of individuals, typically in digital or physical environments
D. The interactions and relationships within a group
E. Complex and advanced in design or function
F. A set of symbols used for phonetic transcription, which represents the sounds of speech
G. Writing systems that use pictograms; these are symbols that represent objects or concepts through visual resemblance
H. A mathematical method used for analyzing data
I. The act of making sounds by a person or animal using the voice
J. A group of mammals that live in the ocean

Task 3 (Viewing & Scanning: Answer the Multiple-Choice Questions)

動画を視聴し、次の質問の答えを、A~Dより選びましょう。

1: What type of communication similarities do sperm whale codas have with human languages?
　A) Random sequences of clicks
　B) Fixed patterns of clicks similar to words
　C) Visual symbols like hieroglyphics
　D) They do not resemble any form of human language.

2: What did the new research reveal about the sperm whale's communication system?
   A) It is primitive and basic.
   B) It lacks a complex structure.
   C) It is sophisticated and structured.
   D) It relies solely on visual cues.

3: According to the researchers, how do sperm whales produce their vocalizations?
   A) At random without any clear pattern
   B) In a limited set of fixed patterns
   C) By mimicking other marine animals
   D) Based solely on their mood and environment

4: What role does artificial intelligence play in this research?
   A) It helps in visualizing whale movements.
   B) It is used to analyze the complexity of whale calls.
   C) It translates whale sounds into human language directly.
   D) It predicts the future behaviors of whales.

Task 4 (Dictation)

動画を音声に注意して視聴し、下線の部分にチャンク（英語数語）を書き込みましょう。

This is what it sounds like when sperm whales communicate.

Those bursts of clicking noises are called codas. It's sounds a bit like Morse code. New research has found their system of communication is more sophisticated than once thought . . . and even has some [1]_____.
Like all marine mammals, sperm whales [2]_____. Their calls are an integral part of this.

Using traditional statistical analysis and artificial intelligence, researchers examined calls made by about 60 whales. They found the vocalizations exhibit [3]_____ and seemingly even a "phonetic alphabet."

Researchers also identified similarities to aspects of other animal communication systems, [4]_____. "So whales don't produce arbitrary

sequences of clicks. They instead intend to produce them in one of a relatively [5] ...."
MIT Professor Jacob Andreas is one of the researchers working on Project CETI.

"So on one hand, you have pictographic systems like ancient Egyptian hieroglyphics, where every word is associated with a different kind of unique picture, and there aren't actually relationships between them. And on the other hand, you have alphabetic systems like English, where there's a much smaller set of pieces that we call letters, that combine to produce all the different words that we see, written down. And so one way of thinking about what we're doing in this new paper, is showing that sperm whale codas are more [6] .... than a pictographic system, which was kind of the picture that we had before . . . that all these different codas that we see are actually built by combining a comparatively simple set of small letter pieces."

Sperm whales, which can reach about 60 feet long and are the largest of the toothed whales, also have the largest brain of any animal.
Researchers found [7] ...., rhythm and tempo of the clicks produced different types of codas. The whales [8] .... of the codas and sometimes add an extra click at the end, like a suffix in human language.

But what exactly are the whales talking about? MIT's Andreas says they're still trying to figure that part out.

"What [9] .... is to link this structure that we're finding to meaning you really need to figure out how the sounds that the whales are producing ground out in their behavior and in their social dynamics."
"And so a big part of the larger Project CETI effort here, is to actually get that behavioral data paired with communication data [10] .... these deeper questions about what it is that the whales are saying."

Task 5 (Reading: Answer the Questions in Japanese)

Task 4 で完成した英語ニュースを読んで、次の質問に日本語で答えましょう。Words & Phrases も参考にしましょう。

Words & Phrases

sperm whales マッコウクジラ（体長は約 20 メートル、体重は約 57 トン。特徴的な四角い頭としわのある暗灰色の皮膚を持つ）／**Morse code** モールス信号／**integral** 不可欠な／**identify** 特定する、明らかにする／**arbitrary sequences of clicks** 無作為なクリック音の連続／**MIT** マサチューセッツ工科大学／**project CETI** (Cetacean Translation Initiative: MIT を含む複数の大学の国際的なプロジェクト。マッコウクジラのコミュニケーションを研究している)／**hieroglyphics** 象形文字／**is associated with ~** 関連付けられている／**toothed whales** 歯を持つクジラ／**suffix** 接尾辞／**figure out** 理解する／**ground out in their behavior** 行動に根ざしている

1: マッコウクジラのコミュニケーションについての新たな研究は、何を明らかにしましたか。

2: マッコウクジラの発声の構造について、研究者たちは何を発見しましたか。

3: MIT の Jacob Andreas 教授は、新しい論文の中でマッコウクジラのコーダについてどのようなことを示しましたか。

4: マッコウクジラのコーダの持続時間とクリックについて、研究者たちはどのようなことを発見しましたか。

5: マッコウクジラの発声とその社会的ダイナミクスの関連性について、今後の難しい研究課題とは何ですか。

Task 6 (Summary)

かっこに英語1語を入れて、動画ニュースの内容をまとめましょう。なお、ヒントになるよう、最初の文字を指定しています。

New research has discovered that sperm whales, highly social marine [m   ], have a more sophisticated communication system than previously believed. Their [v   ], called codas, resemble Morse code and show a complex internal structure similar to a phonetic [a   ]. Using statistical analysis and artificial intelligence, researchers analyzed calls from about 60 whales and identified patterns akin to human [c   ] systems. They are now seeking to [l   ] these vocal patterns to behavioral data to understand the meanings behind the whales' communications.

Task 7 (Writing & Speaking)

本文や Task 6 を参考にして、動物の能力について、自由に英語で数行書いてみましょう。また、ペアで発表をしてみましょう。

Unit 15 New Zealand's Space Industry Shoots for the Stars

YouTube

Task 1 (Guessing & Skimming)

動画を視聴する前に、写真と Key Words を見て内容を推測してみましょう。推測した内容をペアで話し合ってみましょう。

Key Words

1. aerospace facility
2. global hub
3. space exploration
4. commercial space launch
5. debris
6. latitude
7. subsidiary
8. publicize
9. infrastructure
10. regulatory burden

....

....

....

....

Task 2 (Matching)

Key Words の内容を表している英語を下の選択肢 A~J より選び、Key Words の意味を確認しましょう。

1. aerospace facility (　　)
2. global hub (　　)
3. space exploration (　　)
4. commercial space launch (　　)
5. debris (　　)
6. latitude (　　)
7. subsidiary (　　)
8. publicize (　　)
9. infrastructure (　　)
10. regulatory burden (　　)

❑ 選択肢 ❑

A. The investigation of outer space through the use of astronomy and space technology
B. The challenges and obligations companies face due to regulations
C. To make something widely known or to give it publicity
D. Scattered pieces of waste or remains, particularly from space launches or constructions
E. A company controlled by another company
F. A complex dedicated to activities related to space and aviation
G. The geographic coordinate that specifies the north-south position of a point on the Earth's surface
H. The act of sending spacecraft into space for commercial purposes
I. A central point for activities on a global scale
J. The fundamental facilities and systems serving a country, city, or area, essential for industry growth

Task 3 (Viewing & Scanning: Answer the Multiple-Choice Questions)

動画を視聴し、次の質問の答えを、A~D より選びましょう。

1: What is the primary purpose of the Tawhaki National Aerospace Centre?
   A) To serve as a tourist attraction
   B) To conduct scientific research only
   C) To be a key aerospace facility
   D) To maintain its status as a cattle grazing land

2: What advantage does New Zealand's geographical location offer for its aerospace industry?
   A) Proximity to major space exploration bases like Vandenberg
   B) Favorable conditions for placing satellites into specific orbits
   C) The highest number of rocket launches globally
   D) Presence of extensive air traffic

3: What does the U.S. Space Foundation statistic about commercial space launches indicate?
   A) A decrease in commercial space activities
   B) That space launches are solely government-funded
   C) A 50% increase in commercial space launches in 2023 compared to the previous year
   D) A shift of commercial launches to military purposes

4: What is New Zealand's government's goal for the aerospace industry by 2030?
   A) To grow the aerospace industry to $6.2 billion
   B) To maintain the current level of activity
   C) To decrease the industry size due to environmental concerns
   D) To surpass the aerospace industries of neighboring countries

Task 4 (Dictation)

動画を音声に注意して視聴し、下線の部分にチャンク（英語数語）を書き込みましょう。

Welcome to Tawhaki National Aerospace Centre. Once a spot for cattle to graze, this stretch of land on the east coast of New Zealand's South Island is now a key aerospace facility.

It's part of the Pacific nation's plan to become a global hub for advanced aircraft—and space exploration. But before that—New Zealand's got some [1]........................... .... Around the world, the space and aerospace industries are growing—and fast. The U.S. Space Foundation says there were 50% more commercial space launches in 2023 [2]... .

Analysts say New Zealand's location might give it a leg up as it tries to get a larger share of the $600 billion global market. At Tawhaki—there is little air traffic over the spit, launches over water minimize the risk of falling debris, and a latitude deep in the Southern Hemisphere [3] .... satellites in specific orbits.

Four companies, including Boeing subsidiary Wisk Aero, have publicized using the facility to test new technology. Facility officials say that others are there too, but that they can't discuss them [4] ....

The country hosted seven rocket launches last year—making it the fourth-most globally. All were by the U.S.-listed and New Zealand-founded Rocket Lab, [5] .... in New Zealand since 2017. The success of the roughly $2 billion company has helped [6] .... sector here. But New Zealand is still a small player, even relative to its neighbors.

"There's a wide range of space and advanced aviation projects that are really starting to kick along and [7] .... and a lot of value for New Zealand." Mark Rocket is the President of Aerospace New Zealand. "But yeah, we've got a long way to go and we're certainly a long way behind many other countries in the investment and the infrastructure that we need to really grow the industry and support the industry.

In 2019— [8] .... —New Zealand's space industry was worth roughly $1 billion. Comparatively, Australia's space sector is worth around $3 billion annually, while Japan is at $27 billion. New Zealand's government wants to grow its aerospace industry to $6.2 billion by 2030. To do that, it said that it wants to reduce the regulatory burden for launches, [9] .... in the space sector.... Something Rocket says is desperately needed.

"We do [10] .... in the system so we need more support in those entities to make sure that we can bring in international projects and give them a short wait time so that they can get those projects started."

Task 5 (Reading: Answer the Questions in Japanese)

Task 4 で完成した英語ニュースを読んで、次の質問に日本語で答えましょう。Words & Phrases も参考にしましょう。

Words & Phrases

Tawhaki National Aerospace Centre タワキ国立航空宇宙センター／**give it a leg up** 優位性を与える／**spit** 岬／**minimize the risk** リスクを最小限にする／**advanced aviation** 先端航空技術／**orbits** 軌道／**entity** 実在物

1: タワキ国立航空宇宙センターは、どこにありますか。また、そこはかつてどのような場所でしたか。

　　..

　　..

2: ニュージーランドの地理的条件が、航空宇宙産業にどのような利点をもたらしていますか。3点述べましょう。

　　..

　　..

3: Rocket Lab の宇宙工学における昨年度（前年度）の功績は、どのようなものでしたか。

　　..

　　..

4. Mark Rocket は、ニュージーランドの航空産業において、どのような点で他国に遅れをとっていると言っていますか。

　　..

　　..

5: ニュージーランドの政府が航空宇宙産業の成長に向けて設定した目標は何ですか。また、その目標を達成するために必要とされていることは何ですか。

　　..

　　..

Task 6 (Summary)

かっこに英語1語を入れて、動画ニュースの内容をまとめましょう。なお、ヒントになるよう、最初の文字を指定しています。

New Zealand is transforming the Tawhaki National Aerospace Centre into a key facility to become a global hub for advanced [a   ] and space exploration. With the global aerospace industry rapidly growing, the country aims to capture a larger share of the $600 billion [g   ] market. Its location is advantageous for launching [s   ], minimizing the risk of falling debris over water. Despite hosting several commercial [l   ], New Zealand faces challenges like the regulatory burden and needs more investment and [i   ] to compete globally. The government plans to grow its aerospace industry to $6.2 billion by 2030.

Task 7 (Writing & Speaking)

本文やTask 6を参考にして、宇宙工学や宇宙旅行について、自由に英語で数行書いてみましょう。また、ペアで発表をしてみましょう。

....
....
....
....
....

Key Words List

A
- [ ] **activities**   Unit 1
- [ ] **adapt**   Unit 1
- [ ] **aerospace facility**   Unit 15
- [ ] **AI (artificial intelligence)**   Unit 3
- [ ] **AI models**   Unit 3
- [ ] **Antarctic**   Unit 8
- [ ] **anticipate**   Unit 3
- [ ] **availability**   Unit 4

B
- [ ] **behavioral data**   Unit 14
- [ ] **breakthrough**   Unit 10
- [ ] **businesses**   Unit 1

C
- [ ] **cadaveric kidney donation**   Unit 10
- [ ] **carbon footprint**   Unit 11
- [ ] **charging stations**   Unit 4
- [ ] **climate change**   Unit 1, 8
- [ ] **clusters**   Unit 12
- [ ] **cochlear implants**   Unit 6
- [ ] **codas**   Unit 14
- [ ] **combat**   Unit 6
- [ ] **commercial space launch**   Unit 15
- [ ] **compatibility**   Unit 10
- [ ] **conservation**   Unit 9
- [ ] **consumption**   Unit 2
- [ ] **contamination**   Unit 11
- [ ] **controversial**   Unit 7
- [ ] **coral**   Unit 8
- [ ] **coral bleaching**   Unit 13
- [ ] **CS3**   Unit 8
- [ ] **cutting-edge**   Unit 5

D
- [ ] **deaf**   Unit 6
- [ ] **debris**   Unit 15
- [ ] **delicacy**   Unit 7
- [ ] **diagnostic**   Unit 5
- [ ] **dialysis**   Unit 10
- [ ] **dietary habits**   Unit 2
- [ ] **duration**   Unit 14

E
- [ ] **economic alternative**   Unit 13
- [ ] **economic inpacts**   Unit 1
- [ ] **ecosystems**   Unit 8
- [ ] **El Niño**   Unit 8
- [ ] **electric field**   Unit 2
- [ ] **electric vehicle**   Unit 4
- [ ] **embark on**   Unit 11
- [ ] **endangered species**   Unit 7
- [ ] **end-stage renal disease**   Unit 10
- [ ] **expand**   Unit 4
- [ ] **exploitation**   Unit 7

F
- [ ] **facial actuators**   Unit 3
- [ ] **facial expressions**   Unit 3
- [ ] **function**   Unit 9

G
- [ ] **geared towards**   Unit 9
- [ ] **gene therapy**   Unit 6
- [ ] **genetically edited**   Unit 10
- [ ] **get one's foot in the door**   Unit 9
- [ ] **global hub**   Unit 15
- [ ] **global users**   Unit 2
- [ ] **groundbreaking**   Unit 6

H
- [ ] **Hautacam**   Unit 1
- [ ] **healthcare**   Unit 5
- [ ] **high blood pressure**   Unit 2
- [ ] **high-precision**   Unit 5
- [ ] **high-resolution cameras**   Unit 3
- [ ] **hold clues**   Unit 9
- [ ] **human-caused alterations**   Unit 9

I

- [ ] impact   Unit 7
- [ ] in a targeted manner   Unit 12
- [ ] incinerated   Unit 11
- [ ] infrastructure   Unit 15
- [ ] insufficient to fill that need   Unit 10
- [ ] intensify   Unit 13
- [ ] intuitive   Unit 3

L

- [ ] land in a lab   Unit 9
- [ ] lateral flow tests (LFTs)   Unit 11
- [ ] latitude   Unit 15
- [ ] life support   Unit 10
- [ ] limited run   Unit 2

M

- [ ] manufacture   Unit 12
- [ ] marine   Unit 8
- [ ] marine mammals   Unit 14
- [ ] marine reserve   Unit 13
- [ ] mass bleaching event   Unit 13
- [ ] meat alternatives   Unit 7
- [ ] metabolism   Unit 13
- [ ] microalgae   Unit 13
- [ ] mind-blown   Unit 6
- [ ] Mobile World Congress   Unit 5

N

- [ ] no trace of   Unit 7
- [ ] nonverbal communication   Unit 3

O

- [ ] obstacles   Unit 6
- [ ] ocean   Unit 8
- [ ] one and done   Unit 6

P

- [ ] perceived saltiness   Unit 2
- [ ] peruse   Unit 7
- [ ] phonetic alphabet   Unit 14
- [ ] pictographic systems   Unit 14
- [ ] plant-derived ingredients   Unit 7
- [ ] potential   Unit 12

- [ ] prototype   Unit 11
- [ ] publicize   Unit 15

R

- [ ] range anxiety   Unit 4
- [ ] rechargeable battery   Unit 2
- [ ] recipient   Unit 10
- [ ] record   Unit 8
- [ ] recreate   Unit 7
- [ ] recycled materials   Unit 11
- [ ] reduce salt intake   Unit 2
- [ ] redundant   Unit 4
- [ ] regain   Unit 6
- [ ] regulatory burden   Unit 15
- [ ] repair damaged tissue   Unit 12
- [ ] resilient   Unit 13
- [ ] resort   Unit 1
- [ ] reuse   Unit 4
- [ ] robotic   Unit 5
- [ ] run the trial   Unit 4

S

- [ ] safety   Unit 5
- [ ] self-modeling   Unit 3
- [ ] shark habitats   Unit 9
- [ ] silicone skin   Unit 3
- [ ] single-use   Unit 11
- [ ] snow   Unit 1
- [ ] social dynamics   Unit 14
- [ ] sophisticated   Unit 14
- [ ] space exploration   Unit 15
- [ ] starting milestone   Unit 8
- [ ] statistical analysis   Unit 14
- [ ] stimulate   Unit 12
- [ ] subsidiary   Unit 15
- [ ] surgery   Unit 5
- [ ] survival   Unit 1
- [ ] sustainable   Unit 11
- [ ] swath   Unit 13
- [ ] synthetic conditions   Unit 12

T

- [ ] technology   Unit 5
- [ ] telecom boxes   Unit 4

- [ ] **telecom giant**   Unit 4
- [ ] **therapeutics**   Unit 12
- [ ] **toddler**   Unit 6
- [ ] **tourism revenue**   Unit 13
- [ ] **tourists**   Unit 1

U
- [ ] **underwater ecosystem**   Unit 9
- [ ] **underway**   Unit 12
- [ ] **utensil**   Unit 2

V
- [ ] **virgin plastic**   Unit 11
- [ ] **vocalization**   Unit 14

W
- [ ] **wearable**   Unit 5
- [ ] **weekly expedition**   Unit 9
- [ ] **width**   Unit 12

X
- [ ] **xenotransplantation**   Unit 10

Reuters News Agency Reports on Our World
ロイターで学ぶ、環境、健康、AI、サイエンス

2025年1月15日　初　版

著　者© 　小笠原　真　司
　　　　　奥　田　阿　子
　　　　　廣　江　　　顕
　　　　　William　Collins

発 行 者　　佐々木　　　元

発 行 所　株式会社　英　宝　社
〒101-0032 東京都千代田区岩本町 2-7-7
TEL 03 (5833) 5870　　FAX 03 (5833) 5872
https://www.eihosha.co.jp/

ISBN 978-4-269-19050-4 C1082
[製版：ほんのしろ／印刷：モリモト印刷 (株)／表紙：伊谷企画／製本：井上製本所]

本テキストの一部または全部を、コピー、スキャン、デジタル化等での無断複写・複製は、著作権法上での例外を除き禁じられています。本テキストを代行業者等の第三者に依頼してのスキャンやデジタル化はたとえ個人や家庭内での利用であっても著作権侵害となり、著作権法上一切認められておりません。